THE
ARGUS 35MM GUIDE
AND **REFERENCE** BOOK

by
KENNETH S. TYDINGS, S.P.E.

TENTH PRINTING, FEBRUARY 1956

GREENBERG : PUBLISHER

New York

Library of Congress Catalog Card Number: 52–8125

INTRODUCTION

Argus, Inc. can be justly proud of having made and sold more than one million cameras. This very impressive production figure must result from the continued public acceptance and use of the various models because of their inherent ruggedness and fine craftsmanship. Despite any rough handling which beginners may give a camera, the Argus will continue to produce excellent results year after year of use. It is safe to say that many of the top-flight photographers cut their eyeteeth with at least one of the Argus cameras. To help you cut your eyeteeth with your camera, this Guide provides the firm foundation of photographic knowledge to enable you to get good results with the very first roll of film.

The Guide discusses the different Argus models and details their photographic capabilities. The basic pre-settings of each camera control are so presented through illustrations that you will immediately master its use. Both beginner and advanced amateur will profit from the section on the basic lighting and subject fundamentals which are necessary to make a photograph (the Universal L-A-B-S Formula). The beginner, in addition, will welcome the photographic dictionary which explains many of the expressions peculiar to photography. In the final section, various uses for the Argus are described so that you can produce excellent color as well as black-and-white pictures for stereo, portraits, action shots, etc. Several pages of charts and tables serve as a valuable reference source.

The author has no affiliation whatsoever with the Argus Company and his descriptions of the cameras are as objective as those of a disinterested person can be. After reading this Guide, the owner of an Argus will realize that his camera is an instrument capable of far more than just ordinary shooting; it can produce outstanding pictures.

CONTENTS

1. Rapid Results with Your Argus 5
2. S—The Shutter 14
3. A—Aperture (Iris) 18
4. F—Focusing 20
5. E—Exposure 27
6. Loading and Unloading Your Camera 31
7. Wide-Angle and Telephoto Lenses 34
8. Flash with Your Argus 38
9. Useful Accessories 43
   PHOTOGRAPHIC DICTIONARY 45
10. Close-ups and Parallax Control 48
11. Film for Black-and-White Photography 55
12. Filters for Black-and-White Photography 57
13. Processing for Black-and-White Photography 61
14. Color Film 66
15. Color Filters 68
16. L—Light Sources 72
17. A—Angle Arrangement 76
18. B—Balance 83
19. S—Subject Composition 88
20. Existing Light (10X) Photography 91
21. Copying and Microfilming 97
22. Slides and Their Projection 98
23. Stereo and Stereo Projection 101
24. Existing, Flash and Flood Light 106
25. Photomicrography 108
26. Color Balance 113
27. Portraiture 118
28. Medical and Scientific Photography 123

The Argus A-4

With the Argus A-4 Argus, Inc. continues to maintain its tradition for designing cameras that are easy to operate. The controls are large, numerals are clear and easy to read, and the knobs operate smoothly and rapidly. The f/3.5 Cintar is the same as the lens that is used on the C-3. The shutter speeds include 1/25, 1/50, 1/100, 1/200 and B (bulb). The lens is flash synchronized for Class M (#5, #25, etc.) lamps at 1/25 second and at 1/25, 1/50, and 1/100 with Class F (SM or SF) lamps.

The Argus C-3

CHAPTER 1 / **RAPID RESULTS WITH YOUR ARGUS**

Now that you own an Argus, you will want to use it immediately and get good results. To secure quick results without any preliminary knowledge of theory or practice, simply do this:

1. Load the camera with daylight color film as per the instruction sheet, or have a camera store clerk assist you.

2. Set your distance indicator at 18 feet.

3. Set your aperture so that the space between 8 and 5.6 comes opposite the indicating point.

4. Your shutter dial is set so that the 50 is next to the marking line. The C-3 requires a separate setting movement of the cocking lever (down) when you are holding the camera with the lens facing the subject. Do this gently. You will hear a click when the shutter is set. The remaining models have self-cocking shutters that set themselves as you press your release.

5. Hold the camera firmly.

6. Look through your viewfinder. You will see your subject much smaller, but whatever is seen, shows the same area that the camera sees and takes for most distances. At the 18 feet setting, everything from approximately 9 feet to infinity will be in focus. For specific distances, use the chart on pages 9 and 10.

7. Wait for a clear sunny day. With color it is desirable to wait for that type of day when colors will be most brilliant. Colors will photograph best only on a clear day. If the day is dull and overcast, your final picture will also be dull and overcast. You will find that the camera controls described here are correct for a bright day, that is one that will yield the best color. For other conditions, consult an exposure chart or an exposure meter. If the weather is not ideal, you may use your camera indoors or outdoors with its accessory flash unit. Using the flashlamp (bottled sunshine) you can become totally independent of the weather. In using flash, remember that your flash synchronization takes place at certain specific speeds, with 1/25 or 1/30 second recommended for your Class M (#5, #25, #0, #11, etc.) while 1/100 is a safe choice with the Class F (SM, SF) flashlamps.

To use your Argus for flash:

1. Pre-select subject size and subject distance from the chart.

2. Set your distance scale.

3. Choose the aperture for this distance from the chart and set your camera's lens open. You now have pre-set your shutter, your distance and the iris.

4. Now approach your subject to the approximate distance that has been set and observe your subject through the viewfinder or through the rangefinder. With the rangefinder, you can check your distance by moving back and forth until your subject is complete (C-3, C-4). When the image is sharp or you are satisfied that you are reasonably close (FA or 21) view your subject through the viewfinder and wait for the peak of action or expression. Squeeze the release and you have taken your flash picture. Note: Even if you are a few inches before or behind your actual distance setting, do not worry about this slight variance as your depth of field (Chapter 4) adequately compensates for any slight difference of distance.

5. Wind immediately after taking your picture. The C-3, FA winding mechanism does not have an interlock. Therefore, I suggest that you immediately cock your shutter so that there may be no chance for an unintentional double exposure. If you release the shutter when the camera is not in use, be sure to cover the lens with your hand. When you have finished your roll, do not open the camera back because 35mm film must be wound *back* into its cartridge. If in doubt, have your friends show you this step.

6. After opening the back remove the cartridge by pulling out the knob holding the spool in place.

7. Mail your film to the appropriate processing center after carefully addressing the shipping tag and checking your postage.

The returned colored transparencies or prints may be viewed, enlarged, or projected. These instructions are simple and at a minimum. The only judgment required on your part is to wait for a bright, sunny day and to keep the subject within the focus distance from your camera. If these elementary instructions are followed, you can be sure of fine results.

However, your Argus may be used under greatly differing light and distance conditions. The next four chapters will show you how to change the basic settings so that your Argus will be fully flexible and available for all possible changing needs. The time to remember all the picture taking factors is *before* the exposure has been made. As an aid in memorizing these very important points, always recall the word *SAFE* before you are ready to release the shutter.

S—Shutter
A—Aperture
F—Focus
E—Exposure

For convenience of description we shall divide the Argus cameras into two classes:

1. Non-rangefinder models (no longer in production):

(a) *The Argus FA.* The Argus FA is a low-cost 35mm camera which is compact, neat, and convenient. The lens is color corrected, hard coated, and has an f/4.5 speed. Since color is occupying an increasingly important position in modern photography, it can be safely stated that the speed of the f/4.5 lens is sufficient to produce fine results for color when it is used under proper lighting conditions. The model FA has built-in flash, so that indoor flash pictures are easily taken. One may even use it with blue flashlamps outdoors to act as a balancing fill-in.

(b) *The model 21.* This model has very clean modern lines. The lens speed is f/3.5. An f/3.5 lens admits 100 percent more light than an f/4.5 lens. This added speed permits you to take pictures under dimmer light or, on the other hand, will permit you to use a faster shutter speed. The Argus 21 is distinguished by having a built-in "mark finder." The "mark finder" utilizes a unique optical method of outlining the borders of your subject in space so that there will be no doubt at any time of the limits to your subject's area. With this clear outlining of your subject, the chances of poor composition are markedly lessened.

2. Rangefinder models:

(a) *The C-3.* The Argus C-3—the "old reliable"—has retained its position of being at the forefront of the most popular and desirable cameras for almost twelve years. Its ruggedness and reliability have made it a continuing favorite. It was the first low-priced rangefinder camera to incorporate convenient, easy-to-use, built-in flash. The lens is the f/3.5 Cintar which through years of use has always proved to be brilliant and critically sharp.

(b) *The C-4.* The Argus C-4 is the latest addition to the Argus line. The main feature of the C-4 is its unique combined rangefinder and viewfinder—a combination which permits one to focus and compose the picture at the same time, without ever having to shift the eye from one window to another. This time-saver makes picture taking more efficient and quicker. The lens is the new sharp f/2.8 Cintar specifically calculated for contemporary 35mm color photography. Its f/2.8 speed is 60 percent faster in poor light than the f/3.5 of the C-3 or 21.

All the Argus cameras use standard 20- or 36-exposure cartridges.

7

DR. TYDINGS' COLOR OUTDOOR SAFE-SET FORMULA

Lens - 2" Focal Length

	Field Size in Inches Vertical	Approx. Distance
Child Head		
Head	22x15	2.5 feet (.75M)
Head & shoulders	32x21	3.5 feet (.96M)
Three-quarters	45x30	5.5 feet (1.7M)
	63x41	7 feet (2.13M)
Full body	90x60	10 feet (3.05M)
Horizontal-Full body	126x82	14 feet (4M)
	144x96	16 feet (4.6M)

For children: Use all settings for the previous size e.g. a child's full body, vertical equals an adult's three-quarter body size.

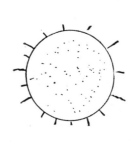

1. Film: Color daylight; Type A or Kodacolor A with No.85B; Ansco Color Indoor with Conv. No.11.

2. Light: Clear day; not harsh.

3. For scenics: Set focus at 18 feet; keep subject at least 10 feet away.

4. For portraits, etc.

A. Choose the subject distance from the chart.
B. Pre-set your rangefinder for your subject distance.
C. Look through the rangefinder or guess your distance, etc., then move back and forth until your image is complete.
D. View and compose your subject.
E. Gently squeeze the release at the peak-of-the-picture.
F. Wind for the next exposure.

E-Effect

F—Focus

A—Aperture

S—Shutter

DR. TYDINGS' OUTDOOR SAFE-SET FORMULA FOR COLOR FLASH

Code:-
- H - Handkerchief; Thin, white linen.
- # - Child's Head.
- § - Head.
- † - Head and Shoulders.
- ‡ - Three Quarters.
- + - Full Body, Vertical.
- ¶ - Full Body, Horizontal.

$$f/16 = f/22+1H = f/32+2H = f/45+3H$$

2" (50mm) Lens:

Outdoor										
	48	1'	#1'6"	§2'2"	3'	4'4"	‡6'	8'7"	+12'	§15'
Kodachrome	85	#2'	§2'7"	†3'10"	†5'3"	7'8"	+10'	¶15'	20'	24'
Ansco Color	55	1'3"	#1'8"	§2'6"	†3'6"	‡5'6"	7'	+10'	¶14'	16'
Kodacolor										

1/30 or 1/25 Sec. 5B, 25B

DR. TYDINGS' SAFE-SET FORMULA FOR INDOOR FLASH

2" (50mm) Lens:

	Guide No.	2H+ f/22	1H+ f/22	22	16	11	8	5.6	4	3.5
ASA										
ASA 80	200	†4'5"	†6'3"	+9'6"	¶12'6"	18'	25'	36'	50'	
40	140	§3'	†4'5"	†6'2"	+8'9"	¶13'	17'	24'	35'	
32	110	§2'5"	†3'6"	‡5'4"	6'10"	+10'	¶13'6"	19'6"	27'6"	
Kodachrome F	90	#2'	§2'9"	+9'	‡5'7"	8'	+11'	¶16'	22'	25'
Kodacolor F	95	#2'	§3'	‡4'3"	‡5'9"	8'7"	+12'	¶17'	24'	27'
Ansco Color Indoor	75	#1'6"	§2'4"	†3'4"	4'8"	‡6'9"	+9'4"	¶13'	18'	21'
SM SF										
ASA 80	110	§2'5"	†3'6"	‡5'4"	6'10"	+10'	¶13'6"	19'6"	27'6"	
40	75	#1'6"	§2'4"	†3'4"	4'8"	‡6'9"	+9'4"	¶13'	18'	21'
32	60	1'3"	#2'	§2'8"	†3'8"	‡5'4"	7'6"	+10'6"	¶15'	17'
82A Kodachrome F	56	1'3"	#1'8"	§2'6"	†3'6"	‡5'6"	7'	+10'	¶14'	16'
82A Kodacolor F	56	1'3"	#1'8"	§2'6"	†3'6"	‡5'6"	7'	+10'	¶14'	16'
UV-16 Ansco Color Indoor	56	1'3"	#1'8"	§2'6"	†3'6"	‡5'6"	7'	+10'	¶14'	16'

1/25 sec.
#5, 25

BACK OF FLASH REFLECTOR

1/25	#5 or #25	Kodachrome, Type F
Head	2½'	f/22 + 2 handkerchiefs
H & S	3½'	f/22 + 1 handkerchief
3/4	5½'	f/16
Full body	10'	f/9

Check your name, address and postage before mailing. The returned picture may be enjoyed by viewing, projection or enlargement.

FLOODLAMP GUIDE—LAMP BESIDE THE CAMERA

Lamp: Floodlamp 1 in suitable reflector or one RFL2
Film: Indoor color, Type F. Filter: 82A

Shutter Speed	Opening	Lamp-to-Subject Distance
1/25	f/2.8	4.6 feet
	f/3.5	3.7
	f/4	3.25
	f/5.6	2.3
1/5	f/2.8	10 feet
	f/3.5	8
	f/4	7
	f/5.6	5
	f/8	3.5

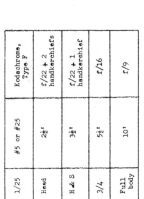

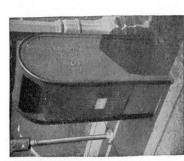

11

The Argus C-4

The dimensions of the negatives or color transparencies are the standard 24x36mm (1″x1½″).

Although a 44mm lens will theoretically cover the film diagonal, all Argus models except the A-4 (which uses a 44mm lens) use a lens of 50mm focal length. The practical use of a slightly larger than necessary focal length insures a positive sharpness and resolution to the very corners of the film.

The Argus cameras will meet the needs of photographers of varying ability. The beginner generally will start with the inexpensive A-4; when his progress requires a design of greater flexibility, he will turn to the C-3 to meet his advancing requirements. Finally, with the C-4 he will find the highest realization of modern mechanical potentialities in an Argus camera.

If you prefer not to make use of the precise exposure variations provided in your C-4, you can "set it on Color-matic," then just wind the film and snap the shutter for each picture—as with the simplest camera.

Color-matic settings are marked in colors for focus, aperture, and shutter speed for any *average* scene in bright sunlight.

When using color film set all three dials on yellow markings. When using black and white film set all three dials on red markings.

12

Inserting a cable release

Speed Setting Ring

When making flash pictures, a shutter speed of 1/25th, marked in green, is suitable for most average subjects.

Individual adjustments are necessary for correct exposure of subjects which are not of the *average* sort or when using other than average emulsion speed films.

Argus Camera	Shutter Speed	Lens Opening	Focusing	Range-finder	Flash	Film & Shutter Interlock	Filter Holder Size	Remov-able Lens
F A	1/25 to 1/150 T and B	f/4.5	Two stage telescoping tube	---	Not in older A's - Built-in for the FA	---	24 mm Series V	---
C 3	1/10 to 1/300	f/3.5	Whole lens unit	Coupled; two window	Built-in	---	18 mm screw-in Series V	Yes
21	1/10 to 1/200 Bulb	f/3.5	Whole lens unit	--	Built-in M7 settings	Yes	21 mm Series V	Yes
C 4	1/10 to 1/300	f/2.8	Whole lens unit	Coupled; one window for range-finder and viewfinder	Built-in MX settings	Yes	33 mm Series V	Yes
A 4	1/25 to 1/200 + B	f/3.5	Front lens	---	MF	Yes	30 mm Series V	---

13

The shutter of your camera may be compared to a water faucet. When the faucet is opened, water will flow. Similarly, when the shutter is opened, light enters your lens. If the shutter remains open a long time, more light will enter through the lens than if the shutter had remained open for only a short time. The volume of light that is available determines whether it is necessary to leave the shutter open for a long or for a short time. When the light volume is very low, you may be required to leave the shutter open for as long as an hour at a time (time exposure). On the other hand, for a sports or action shot a picture may have to be taken in as little as one one-hundredth second because of the fast motion of your subject. With the chart, you can choose the correct shutter speed that is needed. As you will find later, if a choice of speeds is available, the slower speed permits the use of a narrow iris opening with a gain in overall sharpness, while a faster speed produces a shallow depth of field. The proper choice for a correct iris opening may often be an important point in making or breaking the effect of a picture.

A simple shutter speed rule for beginners:

Still (inanimate) subjects may be taken with a slow speed, even *B* or *T*.

Living (animate) subjects require a fast shutter speed of at least 1/50 or as fast a speed as you have. For sports or action pictures use the fastest speed that may be obtained with your shutter.

If, however, you must determine an exact shutter speed for a subject in motion, you can remember what speed to use by knowing the meaning of the series of numbers 25, 5, 25. This basic number means that for a subject 25 feet away, moving at five miles an hour, with a line of motion directly toward and away from the camera's position, the shutter speed need only be 1/25 second. With a 45-degree line of motion, the shutter speed is doubled, while with a 90-degree line of motion, the shutter speed is three times the original 1/25 second. If the speed of the subject is increased to 10 miles per hour, then all numbers are doubled in proportion. As all subject speeds are increased, your shutter speeds are also increased in direct proportion. If, on the other hand, the subject distance is increased to 50 feet, all numbers may be doubled. With a 100-foot distance the figures are quadrupled so that a subject at 20 miles per hour, 100 feet away, with a line of motion toward the camera still will require a 1/25 shutter speed.

SHUTTER SPEEDS FOR MOVING SUBJECTS
LINE OF MOTION

SUBJECT AT 25 FEET	↑↓	↘	⇆
Walking at 5 miles per hour	1/25	1/50	1/100
Children playing	1/50	1/100	1/150
Street activity	1/50	1/100	1/150
Swimmers, skaters	1/50	1/100	1/150
Vehicles at 20 m.p.h.	1/100	1/200	1/300
Football, running	1/100	1/200	1/300
Vehicles at 40 m.p.h.	1/200	1/400	1/600
Tennis	1/300	1/600	1/900
Horse race	1/500	1/1000	1/1500
Airplanes	1/500	1/1000	1/1500

N.B. *When your subject is at 50 ft., multiply all speeds by* $2 (1/100 \times 2 = 1/50)$.

For 100 ft. subject distances, multiply all speeds by 4 $(1/100 \times 4 = 1/25)$.

Cocking the C-3 shutter

So, with the basic 25, 5, 25, you can figure out whatever shutter speed is needed for any subject's motion by simple arithmetic and without having to memorize any chart in full detail.

PANNING

If your highest shutter speed cannot stop the motion of a rapidly moving object from a set position, then the subject's motion may be stopped by "panning" your camera. This means that you swing or move the camera in line with the movement of your subject. When you snap your shutter, the object will be stopped in motion and will be sharp, while the background of necessity will be blurred. While

15

this is not always the best photography, the resulting sharp subject justifies the compromise.

The FA has a single-action shutter; that is, the shutter is released without preliminary cocking. The C-3, the 21, and the C-4 have double-action shutters which must be cocked before they can be released. In the C-4 and the 21, the cocking action occurs simultaneously with the winding of the film. The C-3 has no such interlock, and therefore requires a separate cocking of the shutter.

To set the shutter speed interval, bring the speed number opposite the corresponding indicator mark.

The FA shutter speeds are 1/25, 1/50, 1/100, T and B.

The C-3 shutter speeds are 1/10, 1/20, 1/30, 1/50, 1/100, 1/200 and 1/300 seconds. For B (Bulb) the release must be rotated to the white B. Time exposures may be made with a set-screw type of cable release.

The Argus 21—C-4 shutter speeds are 1/10, 1/25, 1/50, 1/100, 1/200, 1/300, T and B.

To set the shutter for any marked time interval, rotate the ring with the time numeral on it until the desired setting is opposite the indicator. The FA, 21, C-4 cameras have self-cocking shutters which do not require any preliminary pre-setting for release. The C-3 must be pre-set before the shutter can be released.

HAND-HELD EXPOSURES

The 1/50 second setting is the dividing line between recommending exposures with the camera hand-held or supported on a tripod. Since we magnify our pictures by enlargement, projection or viewing, any body vibration or tremor will be transmitted and show on the picture so that the subject will consequently be magnified as a blur. To limit the possibility of blurring with a hand-held camera at speeds of 1/50 second or faster, brace yourself in this fashion. Place your feet so that your toes are approximately four inches apart, your heels about six inches. Hold your camera firmly, take a deep breath and exhale, and shortly after the exhalation you will note that you are at your steadiest. At this point, release the shutter with a smooth even motion.

When no tripod is available, this method has yielded good pictures even at 1/10 second. But at slower speeds than 1/50 second, it is far safer to use a tripod which provides a sturdy support and minimizes camera movement. Practice releasing or cocking and releasing the shutter. Some release levers depress or must be moved

16

considerably before the shutter is actuated. Practice a number of times until you get the pressure and depth of release just right. Action pictures and baby portraits require split second exposures at the peak of action. The shutter must be released immediately, else you may lose in that split second the priceless once-in-a-lifetime expression or rare never-to-be-repeated action.

Practice releasing your shutter so that the camera will remain steady. No matter how steady you may think you are, you will always tend to twist the camera slightly in the releasing direction. If you learn to release your shutter without vibration, your picture at even 1/10 second will enlarge cleanly without any blur. The best place to practice is in front of a large mirror. Stand fairly close and look through the viewfinder as you release the shutter. Any slight movement that you notice would have occurred had you actually taken a picture. The jerking of the camera would have produced an unsharp picture if there had been film in the camera.

CABLE RELEASE

Another important aid for minimizing camera movement is a cable release. When your camera is on a tripod, you must still release your shutter with your finger. Should your finger push against the camera too strongly, some vibration will be transmitted to it through your hand. With a cable release your hand is free and clear of the camera, so that there is no pressure directly against the shutter. A six-inch or longer cable release will suffice for most pictures. Remember that the cable release should be loosely looped for release. If it is stretched taut, your releasing action may still be transmitted to the camera. A loose, unkinked cable release prevents the transmission of any releasing motion.

DELAYED ACTION

If a cable release is not available and you are fearful of vibration, then you can use a self-timer for your Argus. Once you have released the delayed action mechanism, approximately a ten- to fifteen-second delay occurs, and the camera shutter then is released without any vibration. The 15-second delay, in addition, will give you time for getting flash pictures of yourself or by posing in any scenic picture, add that necessary human interest to enhance a picture.

While a faucet is open water will flow through it for any desired length of time. If the faucet opening is narrow, a small amount of water can come through. If the faucet diameter is large, then a greater volume will pour through it. The relationship of the diameter of the faucet to the length of time that it remains open is similar to the relationship of the size of the lens opening to the shutter speed. The shutter speed, in turn, is the amount of time that the lens will remain open. The diameter of a faucet is measured in inches. Photographically, the diameter of the lens must be related to the focal length (lens-to-film distance) at which an infinity image is focused. This ratio of lens diameter to focal length is usually shown as an f/ number.

The f/ number is the relationship of the size of the lens opening to the distance that the light rays must travel before they form a focused sharp image on the film. A small number indicates a wide opening, whereas a high number indicates a narrow opening. The wider the opening, the greater the amount of light that is admitted at a given interval of time. Conversely the narrower the opening, the smaller the volume of light that can enter the camera within the same time interval. For equal exposures, you can have a large opening and a short shutter speed, or a narrow opening with a long exposure. There are different advantages to be gotten from each combination. A wide opening will permit a short exposure, such as is necessary for action pictures. On the other hand, a narrow opening will produce a larger area of subject sharpness in the picture. But, when a sharp image is desirable, but not always possible, you compromise by getting what you can with at least your main subject in sharp detail.

The iris diaphragm of the lens regulates the size of the opening which admits light to the camera. It is in many ways similar to the iris of your eye. Look into a mirror and bring a light close to your eye. As the light is brought closer, you will see that the iris opening narrows; as the light is moved away, the opening widens. You duplicate the narrowing and widening by moving the indicator from the larger to the smaller numbers.

Remember that the narrower the opening of your lens, the greater will be the depth of field. Narrow stops give great depth and wide stops yield very shallow depths. The FA has lens openings of f/4.5, 5.6, 8, 11, 16 and 22. The C-3, 21 lenses start at f/3.5 and narrow down to f/16. The widest opening of the C-4 is f/2.8. An important

18

Aperture Selecting Ring (Illustration 2), a light shade with a Free Iris Diaphragm Control (Chess-United) must be used with the C-3 only to permit a rapid change of iris settings.

Full-stop marking		Relative light increase, if only the iris is widened
f/1	1	These are full stop openings with a 100% difference in light transmission between two adjoining stops.
f/1.4	2	
f/2	4	
f/2.8	8	If the indicator is moved approximately half way between the two markings, the iris is opened ½ stop and the difference in light transmission is increased 50%. Half way between f/5.6 and f/8 produces f/6.3, between f/8 and f/11 is f/9.
f/4	16	
f/5.6	32	
f/8	64	
f/11	128	
f/16	256	

HALF-STOP OPENINGS

f/3.5	1	These specific numbers produce a difference in light transmission of 50% from one mark to another.
f/4	1½	
f/4.5	2	
f/5.6	3	
f/6.3	4½	
f/8	6	
f/9	9	
f/11	12	
f/12.5	18	
f/16	24	
f/18	36	
f/22	48	

N.B. *Everything being equal, if the shutter speed is changed from 1/100 to 1/200, the iris must be widened one stop.*

If the shutter speed is changed from 1/100 to 1/50, the iris is narrowed one stop.

If the shutter speed is changed from 1/100 to 1/75, the shutter is narrowed by ½ stop.

If the shutter is narrowed from f/8 to f/16, the shutter speed is lengthened four times so that 1/100 will be re-set to 1/25.

19

quality of the 2-inch lens of short focal length is its remarkable depth of field. A 2-inch lens at f/4 has the same depth of field as a 4-inch lens at f/8 or an 8-inch lens at f/16. With a 2-inch lens set at f/4, you will be able to get a picture. At f/16, with a lens of longer focal length, to get the same depth of field under the same lighting conditions, your picture will be hopelessly underexposed. In any case the depth of field possible with a lens of short focal length and a wide opening are the all-important factors which make a color picture possible. With a fast shutter speed, your lens opening will have to be as wide as possible to admit more light—at f/3.5 or f/2.8, if available. When your shutter speeds are slow you may narrow your lens opening and still be able to get a far greater depth of field than is possible with a lens of longer focal length. All things being equal, the lens of short focal length has made modern miniature photography possible.

So far you have learned to set your shutter speed and control the variable openings (iris) which admit light to your lens.

CHAPTER 4 / **F—FOCUSING**

Focusing is a process of insuring the maximum amount of image sharpness. To estimate the correct subject-to-camera distance, you may use either a coupled rangefinder, an auxiliary rangefinder, or simply guess the distance. To help you with your guess, you may take advantage of either the depth of field or a hyper-focal distance setting.

Because of the tremendous depth of field of your lens of 2-inch focal length, your images will be sharp at infinity to most middle distances without critical focusing. However, a rangefinder is necessary for distances between 7 and 3 feet. A rangefinder is a simple triangulating device which estimates distances by enabling the viewer to look at the same subject from two different points of view. When the images which are seen from the two viewpoints are brought together so as to form a continuous whole, you have found the distance and your rangefinder is so marked that you may read the exact rangefinder-to-subject distances from the attached measurement scale. The C-3 rangefinder is of the split-field type. This means that the rangefinder image is cut in half as illustrated. When the halves of the subject are brought together to form a continuous image, you are in sharp focus. The C-4's, while similar in principle to the C-3's, have a superimposed-image type of rangefinder. Here you see the whole subject

Two-stage focusing method for the FA.

at all times, but in the center circle of a field of view you will see two
duplicating images when the subject is out of focus. When the lighter
image is brought over the darker image and the two form one continuous subject, then you are in focus. The C-4's rangefinder is unique
in that the rangefinder and viewfinder are combined and are seen
through only one eye window. Your eye can simultaneously check
both focusing and composition so that there is an increasing efficiency
to picture taking. As with all new instruments, it is advisable to
practice using the rangefinder and/or the viewfinder of a camera
without any film in it. The repetition of manipulation will enable you
to get the "feel" of the camera so that the instrument will not be
strange in your hands when you have to use it rapidly. Since the FA
and the 21 do not have a rangefinder. you may use an auxiliary rangefinder for these cameras with excellent results. Pocket type removable
rangefinders are inexpensive and available at most camera stores.

The rangefinder is used according to the Safe-Set Method.

1. Set your rangefinder at the distance of the expected action,
e.g., 10 feet.

2. Set the focus of your camera lens at 10 feet.

3. Ready all your other camera settings (the iris and shutter)
for immediate picture taking.

4. Place your rangefinder conveniently over your camera.

5. Look through the rangefinder and walk forward or back
until the rangefinder indicates that your subject is in focus.

6. With your subject in focus. shift your eye to the viewfinder.
When the subject is at its peak of motion or expression and your
composition is correct, release the shutter.

21

If you must guess your distance or have not the time to use a rangefinder, it is a good idea to know something about depth of field and the hyper-focal distance. We have said that your short focal length lens has a great depth of field. This means that very large areas will be sharp without the need of focusing accurately. Sharpness is a relative term. Reading that everything is sharp from 21 feet to infinity does not mean that your subject is blurred at 18 or 19 feet. This sharpness only means that at a 10-inch viewing distance the eye will be unable to distinguish a separation of two points (dots) if they are 1/100 inch apart.

When you can see the separation between the two points, the continuous tone of your image is no longer smooth and united but will be granular in appearance. To the eye, a granular image does not appear sharp. Thus, to get back to our subject at 19 feet or 18 feet, you will just begin to see the separation of the two dots of your film image. There is no abrupt dividing line from a sharp to a granular (unsharp) image. Rather there is a gradual transition depending upon lens opening, development, etc.

In order to be viewed, 35mm film must be enlarged. To produce an acceptably large image, the subject must be enlarged from at least five to ten times. Contact prints from 35mm film will not show optical granularity if the subject lines are within the 1/100-inch tolerance. When the film is enlarged ten times, the 1/100-inch separation will separate further as two distinct points 1/10 inch apart. Since we can readily distinguish points 1/10 inch apart, an unsharp image which is worthless photographically will result from this enlargement. As all your film must be enlarged, pre-calculate your subject distances and iris openings to be sure that the picture is as sharp as possible. Your rangefinder, for this reason, is highly necessary at the shorter distances. A perfectly focused image will give you a resolution far beyond the required minimum tolerances to produce an image that can be viewed easily or adequately enlarged. The subject of image-point formation is known as the "circle of confusion." Your lenses are calculated for a circle of confusion of 1/1000 the focal length of your lens. This tolerance has proved excellent in result and is easily attained in lens manufacture. When you know beforehand that your subject will need enlargement or projection to immense diameters, then stop down (narrow the opening) at least one or two additional stops to secure greater sharpness than the table indicates. The depth-of-field table may be used if you can either guess your distance ac-

Out of focus with the C-4   In focus

curately or use a measuring tape as an accurate guide. Once you have your subject distance as a reference point, you may use your area of sharpness according to the iris opening.

Related to the depth of field is a table for your hyper-focal distance. When you set your distance (focusing scale) in co-ordination with certain aperture settings, everything will be in focus from half the scale-set distance to infinity. This important table minimizes the need for accurate focusing when certain light conditions permit. An easy way to remember the whole table is by the key number 2, 4, 42. This number means that the 2-inch lens at f/4, focused for 42 feet, will produce an image that is sharp from 21 feet to infinity. At f/8, the setting of 21 feet will have everything in focus from $10\frac{1}{2}$ feet to infinity, etc.

As the table indicates, f/16 with a distance set for $10\frac{1}{2}$ feet will yield a suitably sharp image even if your subject is as close as $5\frac{1}{4}$ feet or as far as infinity. It should be easy to see that this tremendous depth of field minimizes the need for rangefinder focusing. However, if the subject sharpness is placed mostly at infinity (distant landscapes, etc.), you may secure a sharper distance image by leaving the

23

Holding the camera vertically.

Holding the camera horizontally.

rangefinder setting at infinity. For action shots at f/8 with a distance setting of 30 feet, your subject will be in focus from 15 feet to infinity; at f/8 with a setting of 10 feet, your subject will be in focus from 7 to 15 feet.

The FA is focused by first turning the lens mount barrel so that it comes forward to the first position (distance focus). Then move it until it comes forward to its fullest extension.

The non-rangefinder models have a separate viewfinder, a device which indicates the field of view as seen by the camera lens. This viewfinder is generally a reverse Galilean telescope and is adequate from infinity to most near middle distances. The 21 differs from the other cameras in that it optically projects the outline of your subject area into space. With this optical outline, you can easily center the subject and so simplify your compositional problems.

For better composition divide your viewfinder into thirds both horizontally and vertically, and at the intersection of the lines place four dots using a fine pointed pen with India ink. While these dots will not interfere with your viewfinding, they can serve as excellent guide points for your composition.

Caution: The lens of the C-3 and 21 may be separated from the camera and used for enlarging or other photographic needs. If improperly replaced, your rangefinder efficiency will be seriously impaired and may even become inoperative. If this occurs, send the camera to your nearest authorized Argus check station for calibration and adjustment. If you do decide to separate the lens, make a reference

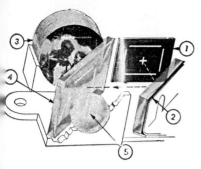

The Markfinder—1. Ground glass 2. Mirror
3. Field of View 4. Semi-silvered mirror
5. Eyepiece
(not on current models)

C-3 Rangefinder effect.

line from the lens through the coupling gear onto the rangefinder gear.

Practice altering your camera settings for different conditions of shutter speed, iris opening and distances so that they will become a matter of "second nature." Try to make every picture as sharp as possible. A sharp picture may be diffused at any later time for a softer effect. But, it is impossible to make an out-of-focus or diffused image critically sharp.

REMOVING YOUR C-3 LENS

1. Set the rangefinder dial wheel to the 3 foot position 2. Unscrew the cap from the idler gear which couples the rangefinder dial wheel to the focus mount. 3. Make a reference line from the focusing mount across the idler gear and onto the rangefinder dial wheel. 4. Remove the idler gear by lifting it straight up. 5. Unscrew lens from front plate of the camera. Do this gently but forcefully if tight.

REPLACING IT

1. Screw lens into the front plate of the camera, turning clockwise until it cannot be turned any further. 2. Turn focusing mount until the reference mark is in position to engage the idler gear (generally the last few teeth). 3. Turn the rangefinder dial wheel until its reference mark is in position opposite the focusing mount. 4. Pick up the idler gear and jockey the reference marks of both the focusing mount and the rangefinder dial wheel until they coordinate with the marks on the idler gear. 5. Install idler gear cap.

25

HYPERFOCAL DISTANCE TABLE
2″(50mm) LENS

Opening	Distance	Over-all Focus
f/ 3.5	52′	26′ to ∞
f/ 4	42′	21′ − ∞
f/ 8	21′	10 1/2′ − ∞
f/ 16	10 1/2′	5 1/4′ − ∞
f/ 22	7 3/4′	4′ − ∞

Distance Focused on	f:3.5 Sharply Focused		f:4 Sharply Focused		f:5.6 Sharply Focused		f:8 Sharply Focused		f:11 Sharply Focused		f:16 Sharply Focused	
	From	To	From	To	From	To	From	To	From	To	From	To
3	2′ 11″	3′ 2″	2′ 10″	3′ 2″	2′ 9″	3′ 3″	2′ 8″	3′ 4″	2′ 7″	3′ 7″	2′ 5″	3′ 11″
3.5	3′ 4″	3′ 9″	3′ 4″	3′ 10″	3′ 2″	3′ 10″	3′ 1″	4′ 1″	3′	4′ 5″	2′ 9″	5′ 1″
4	3′ 9″	4′ 4″	3′ 9″	4′ 4″	3′ 7″	4′ 6″	3′ 6″	4′ 10″	3′ 3″	5′ 3″	3′	6′ 1″
5	4′ 7″	5′ 6″	4′ 6″	5′ 7″	4′ 4″	5′ 10″	4′ 2″	6′ 4″	3′ 11″	6′ 6″	3′ 6″	9′
6	5′ 5″	6′ 9″	5′ 3″	6′ 11″	5′ 1″	7′ 1″	4′ 9″	8′ 2″	4′ 5″	9′ 6″	4′	13′
8	6′ 11″	9′ 6″	6′ 10″	9′ 10″	6′ 5″	10′ 9″	5′ 10″	12′ 8″	5′ 4″	16′ 4″	4′ 8″	32′
10	8′ 4″	12′ 6″	8′ 2″	13′	7′ 6″	15′	6′ 9″	18′ 9″	6′ 3″	28′	5′ 3″	∞
15	11′ 6″	22′	11′	23′	10′	32′	8′ 9″	55′	7′ 9″	∞	6′ 2″	∞
25	16′ 6″	53′	15′ 8″	63′	13′ 9″	162′	11′ 6″	∞	9′ 6″	∞	7′ 6″	∞
50	24′	∞	23′	∞	19′	∞	15′	∞	11′ 9″	∞	8′ 9″	∞
100	32′ 2″	∞	29′ 6″	∞	23′	∞	17′ 4″	∞	13′ 2″	∞	9′ 5″	∞
∞	47′	∞	41′	∞	29′	∞	20′	∞	15′	∞	10′	∞

Now that the mechanics of picture taking have been described, all that remains is for you to integrate this knowledge and prepare to take a picture.

You now know how to set your shutter and iris, but you must know which settings are to be used. There are three methods of determining the proper camera settings for normal lighting conditions.

1. Every roll of film is packaged with an instruction sheet. On this sheet, you will find recommendations for shutter and iris settings for different light conditions. If you follow these recommendations, you will definitely get properly exposed pictures. Remember that the manufacturers take great pains to insure the accuracy of their published information.

2. There are always three factors in determining your camera settings: Film, shutter speed and iris. The exposure chart in this chapter standardizes the setting procedure so that the only variable will be your iris opening. And, to make your choice easy, the different iris openings are derived by the use of simple arithmetic. First choose the number for the correct light conditions and multiply it by the suitable subject classification number. The product of the multiplication will be your iris setting. For example, if you are using film with an ASA 50 and a shutter speed of 1/100 second, then when your subject is average (Class 3) and multiplied by hazy sky lighting (Class 2), the result will be 6. If you set your iris at 6.3, your exposure will be "on the button." Practice a number of times for different subjects and lighting conditions until you have mastered the chart. While this chart gives you iris openings for set shutter speeds only, you can change the settings at will since you can increase your shutter speed by opening your iris in proportion so as to maintain the same volume-time relationship of light. The f/number chart of Chapter 3 will show you the different shutter speeds for proportionate iris opening changes. If you know what speed is needed, then you can open and close the iris from the table number and still maintain the correct exposure.

3. The photo-electric meter is an accepted standard for accurate measurements in indicating correct exposure. While a chart may be used for outdoor settings, only the photo-electric meter is recommended for use with artificial lighting or even outdoors where extreme accuracy is needed for color work.

There are two types of photo-electric meters.

a. *The incident light type.* This meter measures the light that is falling on a scene or a subject. The incident type generally has a collecting sphere (like half a table tennis ball), light masks or great teen type hoods which take a reading by pointing these collecting devices at the camera. The collectors are used to integrate any varied strengths of light reaching them so that the readings are very accurate and are set at the mid-point of a gray scale. The sphere also minimizes the possibility of two eye readings when a spotlight or any other intense light source shines directly on the subject.

b. *The reflection type.* The reflection type measures the amount of light reflected from the subject. It is pointed at the subject for an intensity reading. However, a gray card must be used with this type of meter for accurate results. Because gray is a neutral tone, you will automatically photograph your blacks and whites in their correct tonal differences. If a gray card is not used, then you can see that different reflected readings will result from dark or light subjects. Since both readings cannot be correct, you must do some mental calculation to figure out a new middle value that you hope will give the correct result. The only precaution when using a gray card is to be certain that it is large enough for a reading (point the meter at the card from at least a ten-inch distance) and so be assured that only the reflection from the gray card will influence the meter. In addition, be sure that your body is not blocking any light from its source. Bend your body away or take a knee bend so that your hand is holding the meter free and clear. With these precautions your meter readings can yield excellent results.

With both types of meter there is still some judgment required on your part. For dark subjects the iris may be opened a half stop, while with very light subjects the iris may be closed one half stop below the indicated scale readings.

The exposure factors for flashlamp and flashtube are quite different from those determined by either of the above-mentioned methods. Every flashlamp or flashtube is supplied with an exposure guide number chart by the manufacturer. This chart provides you with a guide number to be used with certain speed films at definite shutter speeds. Since you know your film and shutter speeds, the only remaining unknown is again the iris opening. The iris opening is found by simply dividing the subject distance into the specfic guide number. If, for example, your flashlamp has a guide number of 110 with an ASA 40 film at 1/100 of a second when your subject distance is 10 feet, then you divide 110 by 10 to get an answer of 11. The iris opening of your lens is now se. at f/11. If a subject is 20 feet away, then the iris opening will be f/.5. If your guide number is 56 and your flashlamp-to-subject distance is 6 inches (½ foot), then divide the ½ into the 56 and the indicated opening will be f/112. Since your camera iris generally is narrow only to f/22, then you must use a number of layers of handkerchiefs or white linen cloth to reduce the light intensity of your flash so that it will be correct for your minimum lens opening. This is further explained in Chapter 8.

Standardize with one flashlamp so that you know its characteristics well. With standardization will come a uniformity of results so that you will be able to concentrate on your subject. Finally, I should caution you again to hold your camera firmly and learn to push the shutter release lever gently so that you will not jar the camera.

Exposure Rules

Black and white film: Expose black and white film for the shadows, but develop for the highlights.

Color film: Color film should be exposed for the highlights, but precautions must be taken to assure adequate shadow detail by lighting the shadows with a 3 or 4 to 1 ratio because of the low contrast limitations inherent with most color emulsions.

SIMPLIFIED OUTDOOR EXPOSURE CHART

Film: Outdoor Color—A.S.A. 10
#85C Filter with Indoor Color

B & W—A.S.A. 80
Shutter Speed 1/100

Shutter Speed —1/25th

45° Light Angle to Subject	4—Sunny Strong shadows	3—Bright Soft shadows	2—Cloudy	1—Dull
4 - Wide, clear open spaces	16	12	8	4
3 - People, trees, architecture in outdoor middle distances	12	f/9 or **COLOR** Basic recommended setting 1/50th at 6.3	6	3
2 - Average subjects; open street, near distances	8	6	4	2
1 - Shaded street	4	3	2	1

For normal subjects, normal conditions, normal areas.

Use 1/2 stop wider for dark subjects, etc.

Narrow 1/2 stop for light subjects, etc.

Loading the camera means getting the camera ready for picture taking with fresh film. This operation is very simple with all Argus cameras. The film which is to be loaded in the camera is packaged in standard 35mm cartridges which may be purchased almost anywhere in the world. These cartridges permit camera loading in daylight. While your film may be camera loaded in full daylight, I recommend that the loading procedure take place in subdued light. If no subdued light is available, turn your body so that when the camera is in front of you, it will be away from the light source and you can finish your loading operation in this position. The illustrations demonstrate the loading procedure.

Be sure that the locking catch for the camera back is securely fastened. If you don't depress the retaining spring underneath the locking catch, you may find that the back will suddenly fly open, at the most inopportune time, and spoil all the film which you have exposed with such great pains. Be sure that the perforations engage the sprockets. If this is done, the film automatically winds itself properly onto the take-up spool. In addition, the film will automatically center itself over the back masking frame.

When you thread the end of the film into the slot of the take-up spool be sure that the end is inserted far enough to make your film secure. If it is not secure, you will find that at some time during the course of winding the film may slip. When your film slips, your exposure spacing will not be accurate and the film will have cinch marks which will enlarge as scratches. A thin piece of foam rubber placed on the under side of the camera back will keep the cartridge secure as you unwind the film.

When you have aligned your film on the spindle, the edge of the film must be perfectly parallel with the edge of the film mask. If it is not, your film will start unwinding at an angle onto your take-up spool. When the twelfth or thirteenth exposure is made, the lack of spool alignment will cause a distorted picture which will have friction and cinch marks.

After closing the back of your Argus, the equivalent of three frames should be wound off before you start to take pictures. This is done by winding the film until the exposure counter moves to the next number and stops turning. Repeat this operation twice. Turn your exposure counter to the number 1 for the C-3 and FA. The Argus 21 and

31

Film secure in take-up spool and cartridge in its chamber.

Winding knob, exposure counter to the left.

Remove the back.

LOADING YOUR ARGUS

FA

1. Wind film advance knob until it stops. 2. Open camera by depressing the catch at one end of the camera. 3. Pull out rewind knob. 4. Thread end of film into the slot on the take-up spool. 5. Pay out film and drop cartridge into its chamber. Push rewind knob in. 6. Replace the back of the camera; secure the locking catch. 7. Depress the film catch, start film winding, release film catch and continue winding until knob stops. Repeat this three times. 8. Set exposure counter to "0" by turning it counter-clockwise. You are ready.

C 3

1. Wind film advance knob until it stops. 2. Open the camera by pressing locking catch. 3. Pull out rewind knob and proceed as with FA.

21 - C 4

1. Wind film advance until it stops. 2. Turn locking catch on the bottom of the camera to "open". 3. Slip back off the camera. 4. Pull out rewind knob. 5. Thread end of film under the friction roller. 6. Pay out film and drop cartridge into its compartment. Push rewind knob in. 7. Replace the back; turn the locking catch to "close". 8. Release the shutter and wind the knob until it stops. Do this for a total of three times. 9. Set the exposure counter, at "0" for 36 exposures or 20 for 20 exposures, by turning it clockwise to the index mark. It will show the number of exposures remaining. 10. You are ready for your first picture.

C-4 have an interlock to prevent double exposures. Therefore, you must release your shutter after your winding key stops. The procedure is: Turn the winding key until it stops and release your shutter; then wind again, release your shutter; wind again, and set the exposure counter at number 20 or 36 depending on the number of exposures in the camera. The indicator tells how many exposures are left.

Keep in mind that most 35mm negatives or transparencies are enlarged for viewing, and that the slightest scratch or pin mark on your negative will become noticeable and distracting. Since your 35mm negatives require exacting treatment, start your precautions by loading the camera correctly.

UNLOADING

Your exposure counter will show you when you have made all your exposures.

Your 35mm film is different from your usual roll film spool. There is no paper backing because the extra thickness would add a tremendous bulk to your roll spool. Instead, there is a light trapped cartridge which permits rewinding your film back into the original cartridge after all the exposures have been made so that you can safely take your film out of the camera in daylight.

When you have turned the rewind knob in the indicated arrow direction for some time, you will find that there is a sudden loss of tension and you will hear or feel the end of the film leaving the take-up spool and sliding across the film aperture into the magazine. Another simple way to determine when the film is completely rewound is to observe a moving part on the outside of the camera. For example, on most cameras the winding knob will turn backwards while the film is being rewound and will stop turning completely when the beginning of the film comes off the spool. At this point you may open your camera safely.

If you have torn the film from the spool by force winding at the end of the roll, it will be necessary to go into a dark room, open your camera, remove the cartridge and take it apart so that you can secure the last portion of your film to the center core with scotch tape. Then, replace the core in the outer shell of the cartridge and finally snap on both sides. You can wind your film by hand or by replacing and winding the cartridge in the camera. Be sure that your movement is smooth for winding or rewinding your film. A jerky motion will produce friction, scratches and cinch marks.

The Argus FA and C-3 do not have automatic interlocks to prevent double exposures. Therefore, with the FA wind your film immediately after taking your exposure; with the C-3 and FA wind your film and cock the shutter.

The 21 and C-4 do have automatic interlocks which prevent double exposures. With these cameras, you should also wind your film immediately after taking your picture so that your camera will always be ready for the next picture.

FILM TYPE INDICATOR

The C-3 has a film-type indicator dial on the back of the camera. Set this dial for the type of film that is being used. It is startling to find out how poor your memory is from week to week. Unless you set the indicator, you may be guessing about the film speed or type of film that is currently in your camera. If your camera does not have this aid, tear the name from your film box and place it in your camera case before you insert your camera. This will serve as your reminder as to the type of film that you have in the camera.

Before you are ready to take your first pictures, get a cartridge from a friend or camera dealer and let him help you load your camera and, at the end of the roll, unload it.

Argus Telephoto and Wide Angle
lenses.

Picture with a Wide-   Picture with a Normal   Picture with a Telephoto
angle ACL   Lens   ACL

Normal and Tele-Sandmar's Effect
(Inside Rectangle)

Many times, a change of focal length is desirable to produce a change of perspective and the change of pace in your pictures. A wide-angle lens shows a wider area from the same viewpoint than does the regular prime lens. A telephoto lens on the other hand, while it covers a smaller picture area, enlarges the relative size of the subject image. So while you see less with a telephoto lens, the subject is much larger than usual. The illustrations demonstrate the effects of a wide-angle and a telephoto lens as compared to the area covered by the regular prime lens.

Argus, Inc. now manufactures a true prime wide-angle lens of 35mm focal length, $f/4.5$ for the Argus C-3. The lens couples directly to the C-3 rangefinder so that you focus with it in the same manner as with the normal lens. However, since the angle of view is approximately $65°$, the matching viewfinder must be used to show the larger area that it includes when the subject is composed. The increase in angle also increases the depth of field so that if the lens is set for color at $f/6.3$ and focused at $12'$, everything will be in acceptable focus from $6'$ to infinity. As long as you can judge that your subject is $6'$ or beyond, simply compose and shoot.

Slip-on accessory telephoto and wide-angle lenses are definitely not recommended for Argus cameras because of optical interference and inferior quality of pictures resulting. However, Wide-Angle and Telephoto Lenses manufactured by Argus are definitely recommended, and the C-3 owner is encouraged to interchange them freely at will, without fear of difficulty or injury to camera.

Telephoto Lenses. It is possible to emphasize the size of the subject by the use of the telephoto lens. It enlarges the subject, but a smaller area is included in the picture. Since the enlargement ratio is approximately 30 percent, which is not a very material increase in image size, it is still the only telephoto lens available. Very often, however, this slight enlargement will make a picture unusual. A coordinated telephoto viewfinder mask is available and must be used for your telephoto lens because of the change in the subject size.

The construction of the auxiliary compound telephoto or wide-angle lens is such that your exposure remains the same as if no addition had been made to your regular lens. While no exposure increase is necessary with either lens, it is best to stop down to $f/5.6$ or $f/8$ for satisfactory definition and resolution.

For the best method of taking a series of pictures with these

36

Wide-angle Lens

1. Increases the angle-of-view from the same camera position.

2. Shows a larger amount of total background; each background subject is much smaller.

3. Increases the apparent size of foreground subjects; increases the apparent depth of the foreground.

4. Shorter focal length increases the depth-of-field at equivalent openings.

5. A large image requires a short camera to subject distance.

6. Increased depth-of-field allows the use of wider openings for poor light color exposures.

7. Necessary for interiors; or where space is cramped.

Telephoto Lens

1. Decreases the angle-of-view from the same camera position.

2. Decreases the total background area but increases the size of each individual subject.

3. Increases the subject size in relationship to the proportions of the background.

4. Increases the working distance separating the subject from the camera.

5. Longer focal length decreases the depth-of-field.

6. Narrow lens openings necessary for increased depth-of-field.

7. Needed to bridge space where a camera cannot be set up, e.g. sports, rivers, mountains, etc.

EASY TO INSTALL Simple, four-step installation:

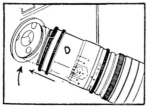

1 Screw telephoto lens into front plate of camera.

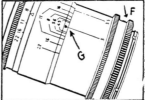

2 Turn Lens Collar and line up the "3" foot marking on the lens barrel with the Focusing Scale Arrow.

3 Turn Range Finder Dial Wheel to "3" foot marking on dial. Then drop Idler Gear between Range Finder Dial Wheel and Lens Focusing Mount.

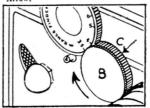

4 Screw Gear Cap into Idler Gear (C). Idler Gear is now locked in place and the telephoto lens is coupled to the range finder.

A reference mark to simplify removing and replacing the C-3's lens.

A true Telephoto Lens—The Tele-Sandmar.

lenses, observe the technique of the motion picture when you see a movie or are watching television. You will see how the first scene of a play generally establishes the locale. This is usually done with a wide-angle or long-distance shot. Once the setting has been established, the attention is drawn to an area or a group of individuals. For most middle distances, your regular lens may be used. Finally, the center of interest in the scene is established with the use of a close-up taken with a telephoto lens. This intermixing of wide-angle, normal and telephoto shots provides the variety and change of pace which make for a story of continuing interest. If you wish to do a story on your town, your industry or your family, write a short scenario of the important points to be photographed. Then to guide yourself when on location, break down each scene into a long-distance, medium and close-up shot so that your story will have both direction and pace.

An interchangeable true telephoto lens for the C-3 only has been recently available. It is a 2x, 100mm focal length, f/4.5, has click stops, couples, and focuses to the C-3 rangefinder from 3 feet to infinity. The Tele-Sandmar, in being changed for your regular lens, requires careful handling. If you do decide to remove the regular lens, paint two reference marks so that the gears will always mesh properly (see illustrations).

CHAPTER 3 / **FLASH WITH YOUR ARGUS**

Ours is an age of bottled, packaged and portable sunshine (flashlamps and flashtubes). It is indeed fortunate that this type of light exists today, else most of our indoor action pictures—whether in

38

black and white or in color—could not have been taken. Color especially requires tremendous amounts of light and the only dependable and readily available source is the flashlamp or the flashtube.

A flashlamp consists of magnesium or magnesium aluminum alloy in a very fine wire form (Class M) or in a pill paste form (Class F). It may have the conventional house lamp shape or, as recently modified, it may be condensed to the size of a walnut. When approximately a 4½ volt electrical current as supplied by small dry cell batteries courses through the flashlamp, the aluminum compound in the bulb flares up for a tiny fraction of a second. Although this flash seems instantaneous to the eye, there is a short time required for the compound to heat up to the flashing point. There are two classes of lamps available with different flare-up time delays: Class F and Class M. The Class F lamps are fast acting, the delay being only five milliseconds (1/200 second) and the complete flash peak duration is also 1/200 second. The Class M lamps are medium acting with an ignition delay of 20 milliseconds (1/50 second) and here the flash peak duration is 1/50 second.

Since the flashlamp can be used just once, inventors have tried to produce a source of flash lighting that will yield a large number of flashes without burning up. The results of their experiments is the electronic flashtube. This type of flash consists of a rare gas (bottled under pressure in a glass tube) which glows brightly only when a high voltage current courses through the tube. The duration of the glow is much shorter than in the flashlamp. The duration has been as little as 1/5000 seconds, but the latest units are designed for a flash duration of 1/1000 second. The newer units, one example of which is the Mighty Midget, in addition operate on a low 450 volt circuit. The only drawback to the flashtube is the tremendous amount of energy required to give the same light output as is possible with the flashlamp. In order to produce a large amount of energy, the more powerful flashtubes are heavy and cannot be carried about your person easily. If they are portable, their color guide number is very low. For these reasons, while most flashtubes produce at least 10,000 flashes without burning out, they are still not too practical. Moreover, flashtubes cannot be used at a distance greater than 10 feet for a well lighted, evenly exposed picture; their color temperature is difficult to match with an appropriate color film; and the light portable models are too weak, while the powerful units are of the heavy studio type (Kodatron).

The Class F lamps (SM or SF) are ideally balanced for indoor

Kodachrome Type A and do not require a light-balancing filter. If Ansco color is used, an 82A filter must be used. The proper filters for each light source are listed in Chapter 11.

Both the flashtube and the flashlamp require precise timing for maximum flash effect. Taking flash pictures with any Argus camera is a very simple matter. The FA has a detachable flash unit which plugs into the side of the camera. No flash adjustment is necessary. Caution: Do *not* place the flashlamp in the flash unit until the latter is attached to the camera. If the flashlamp is placed in the flash unit beforehand it will go off and you will have absolutely no compensation for one blown lamp. After taking the picture, press the lamp ejector and discard the used lamp. Don't run the risk of burning your fingers by grasping a hot lamp.

Class F lamps synchronize at any speed with the FA. Class M lamps synchronize only at 1/25 second (colored green on your speed dial). Electronic tubes synchronize at any speed.

The Argus C-3 also has a plug-in flash unit. It is as easy to attach as plugging a radio into your wall socket. There are no wires or adjustments. To use the C-3 flash unit, remove the camera case. Plug adjustments can be made which will permit you to fit the flash unit through the camera carrying case.

With the C-3, Class F lamps will synchronize at shutter speeds of 1/100 or over. Class M lamps synchronize at 1/25 or 1/30. Electronic flash is used with a 5ms. delay socket at Class F settings.

The Argus 21 flash unit clips into the top of the camera. The square black dot on top of the camera permits adjusting of the ignition delay for different classes of flashlamps. Use the thumb and forefinger to grasp the adjusting black button and turn it left or right with a twisting motion as in using a key. Don't try to move the button with one finger.

With the 21, Class F lamps are used when the *F* is showing. Class M lamps are synchronized when the *M* is visible. Electronic flash should be used with a 5ms. delay plug at the *F* setting.

The flash adjustment for the C-4 is at the back of the camera. When the letter *M* is seen, it is set for the medium action flash; the letter *F* sets the shutter for the Class F lamp. Electronic flash is used with a 5ms. delay socket at the Class F settings.

Note: C-3 and C-4 late models are now synchronized for strobe.

In reading a flash guide number table, you may note that the guide number for Class M lamps up to the speed of 1/50 is always the same. The guide number changes after 1/50 for each increase in shutter speed. Similarly, the Class F number is the same for all speeds

40

up to 1/100 second and then changes abruptly for each shutter speed increase. A choice of speed range or synchronization will do much to help your picture. The I-G-A-S Formula demonstrates the need for balancing your lighting in order to meet the relatively low contrast insensitivity of your emulsion. If the amount of light provided by your flashlamp is taken at one unit, then your background light must also provide one unit to have a 1:1 ratio. However, your background light of one unit does not necessarily have to be flash; it may be a floodlight. Assuming that it is a floodlight, then the location on your floodlamp is directly related to the shutter speed. At 1/25 second the floodlight may be placed further away than at 1/100 second, because the shutter remains open four times as long. The further back your light is placed, the more even is the illumination and the less noticeable will the heat problem be from the glowing floodlamp. In a similar manner, if you are using your flashlamp on a camera as a fill-in for an outdoor picture, the outdoor scene may be perfectly exposed at 1/25 second while at 1/100 even though the flash intensity remains the same, the general scene will be underexposed. Therefore, even if you are given a choice of speeds for a single guide number, the selection should be made with an understanding of the complete lighting problem for the scene rather than for just the one flash in the background.

Note: Class F means fast action and Class M signifies medium action. The names SM and SF have confused the public because both are Class F lamps.

When any dimly lighted activity is being photographed, flash is a must to stop the action. Presuming that color film is being used, you must realize that at this point of our technical development, color film emulsions are relatively slow and each exposure requires huge amounts of light to secure any fairly rapid exposure such as 1/50 second. Flash is the only source of light that can supply the quantity and swift "wallop" of light necessary to produce short exposures.

With a properly synchronized flash unit, your Argus is independent of any light condition. The simplicity of synchronized flash approaches the dream of both amateur and professional for a foolproof, push-button form of photography. If the beginner uses only SM or SF lamps with indoor color and ⚡5B or ⚡25B lamps with outdoor color, then no light balancing filters are needed over the camera lens. In addition, if you use the Safe-Set Formula from Chapter 1 and tape the information onto your reflector, you will avoid all fuss and fumbling so that your attention will be devoted to only one thing—taking the picture!

41

The C-3 set for Flash

The Dual-Purpose Flash Holder for bayonet and standard lamps.

The C-4 set for Flash

An auxiliary clip is most helpful for holding either a wide-angle, telephoto, flash, or any additional speed light unit.

FLASH SYNCHRONIZATION

Camera	Class M	Class F	Strobe
F A	1/25 only	1/25 to 1/150	With special timer or relay delayed strobe
C 3	1/30	1/20 to 1/100	With special timer or relay delayed strobe
21 and C 4	Lever or dial on M	Lever or dial on X	With special timer or relay delayed strobe

Your basic camera provides at least 90 percent of the requirements for most picture taking. However, there are occasions when an Argus might be adapted to meet unusual conditions. As an example, the taking of extreme close-ups necessitates a supplementary lens accessory because the camera focuses to only 3½ feet. Naturally, when you must use any aid other than the basic camera, you have an accessory. Accessories are many in number and, no matter how important they may seem at the moment, are used only once or twice a year. If you think you must purchase an accessory, be sure that you not only will need it now but will use it frequently. Therefore, learn to use what you have and you will find that most of the time you can take and will get pictures.

However certain stock accessories and additions to the bare camera have become accepted through the years as useful adjuncts for good picture taking. These include a light shade, cable release, self-timer, tripod, etc. There may be as many as nine:

1. A filter holder. This is the basic unit which will hold all the other lens accessories. Therefore, it is important that it be secure and not wobble. If there is any bit of wobble or play, your filters and close-up lenses will not be mounted flat (parallel) in relationship to the film, but will be set at a distorted angle. The prism effect produced by the distortion will invariably produce a poor picture. So be certain that the filter holder you use is secure.

2. Portrait or other Proxar Lens. These should be first quality, perfectly centered, ground and polished lenses.

3. Retaining ring.

4. Diffusion disc.

5. Retaining ring.

6. Filters. Filters must be ground and polished to high standards of parallelism. A flat and parallel lens will not produce image distortion.

7. Retaining ring.

8. Polarizing filter.

9. Lens hood (also acts as a retaining ring).

When all the items are used, the above is the correct sequence for attachment. But, you may use 1, 2, 3, 8 or 9, or 1 and 9. With this sequence, loss of light is negligible and distortion is reduced to a minimum. However, the use of more than two optical lenses is not recommended because the increased length of your accessories may

Bulk Film Winder

Argus Projector

Self-Timer

act as a shielding tube so that the corners of your negative can be cut off. Each retaining ring must be correctly sized to hold each portrait, filter, or polarizing disc in proper parallel alliance. Finally, check each filter and disc for proper thickness. If they are too thin, their loose fit in the filter holder or retaining ring will cause them to lean sideways when the accessories are placed upon the camera lens and the camera is tilted slightly. The leaning will cause prism distortion and must be avoided.

ATTACHING ACCESSORIES

Accessories are fitted to the camera lens barrel by either of two methods:

Non-interchangeable (push-on nesting; combinable)

    1.   Fits only one specific lens diameter.

    2.   Compact; one attachment nests into another.

    3.   Easily slips on and off.

Interchangeable (Series V, VI, etc.)

    1.   One series set will fit any specifically fitted rear filter holder of a similar series.

    2.   Discs, retaining rings, etc., are interchangeable.

    3.   Series sizes are determined by lens diameters, e.g., $\frac{3}{4}''$ to $1\frac{3}{16}''$, Series V; $1\frac{1}{4}''$ to $1\frac{21}{32}''$, Series VI, etc.

44

PHOTOGRAPHIC DICTIONARY

This brief dictionary has been prepared to serve as a convenient source of reference for the new camera owner.

ABERRATION—Distortion in the lens.

ACID—Chemical used to stop development.

ADAPTER—Converting unit attached to the lens.

ALKALI—Chemical used to accelerate development.

ALUM—Chemical film hardener which prevents softening, reticulation, and scratching.

ANASTIGMAT—Flat, distortionless, straight-line image.

ANGLE OF VIEW—Subject area seen by a lens in all directions.

ANGLE SHOT—Picture from an unusual angle.

ANHYDROUS—Without water.

APERTURE—Lens opening allowing image-forming rays to enter camera.

ARTIFICIAL LIGHT—Light other than sunlight.

A.S.A.—American Standards Association. Systematizes materials, procedures, techniques, etc.

AUXILIARY LENS—Extra lens attachment to change the function of the regular camera lens.

BETWEEN-THE-LENS SHUTTER—Blades or leaves of the shutter widen to open, then completely close to make an exposure. Located between the lens elements.

BLOWUP—An enlargement.

BOUNCE LIGHT—Light method using walls and ceilings to reflect light.

BRIGHTNESS RANGE—Permissible light-to-dark difference possible for subject, negative, or positive.

BULB EJECTOR—Device for removing hot flashlamps.

BULB EXPOSURE—Picture taken with the shutter set at **B**.

BULK FILM WINDER—Economical device for winding your own individual cartridges from larger rolls.

CABLE RELEASE—Wire, shutter-releasing device which enables you to take pictures without touching the camera. Cable releases may be used five or more feet from the camera.

CAMERA—Light-tight box, having sensitive film on the inside and a light-admitting device (lens) at the other end.

CAMERA, PLANAR—Single-lens camera.

CARTRIDGE, STANDARD—Regular 35mm daylight-loading film-holder which may be purchased anywhere.

CHROMA—Purity of a color mixed with gray.

CIRCLE OF CONFUSION—Area in which two dots appear as one. Two separated dots will appear as one when separated by 1/100 inch at a 10" reading distance.

CLOSE-UP—Picture taken closer than eight (8) feet from subject.

COATED LENS—Anti-reflection deposit on lens surface to permit more light to pass.

COLOR BLIND—Film sensitive only to blue or violet light.

COLOR CONTRAST—Distinct separation of different colors.

COLOR CORRECTED—Optically balanced to assure similar sharpness of all colors.

COLOR HARMONY—Combination of colors producing a pleasing effect.

COLOR SENSITIVITY—Varying color response of different films.

COLOR TEMPERATURE—The degrees K° refer to the comparative color changes that occur when a black body (iron) is heated. A low number indicates a more reddish color; a higher number, a bluer shade. Most important for natural color film.

COLOR TEMPERATURE METER—Device which measures color temperature, establishes color balance.

COMPLEMENTARY COLORS—Any two combined colors other than the primary.

COMPOSITION—Orderly arrangement of a picture to produce the most pleasing effect.

CONDENSER—Light-concentrating lens.

CONTRAST—Comparison of light to dark.

CONTRASTY—Abrupt difference of light-to-dark tones.

CROPPING—Trimming a picture for the most effective composition.

CUTTER—Special slicer for cutting film or print with clean or deckled (wavy) edges.

DAYLIGHT TANK—Special developing tank which permits negative processing in full light.

DEFINITION—Sharpness.

DELAYED ACTION—Automatic shutter release mechanism operating after a predetermined interval without human effort. Permits you to photograph yourself.

DENSITOMETER—Measures thickness of exposed and developed film silver deposit.

DEPTH OF FIELD—Area of satisfactory image sharpness. Distances at different apertures are usually supplied in table form.

DEVELOPER—Chemical which blackens only exposed portions of film.

DEVELOPMENT—Complete process of developing, shortstopping, and fixing exposed film.

DIFFUSION—Light which is scattered. Reduces sharpness of image.

DOUBLE EXPOSURE—Taking two pictures on one negative. May be accidental, or intentional for special effects.

EASEL—Paper-holding device for enlarging.

ELEVATOR TRIPOD—Convenient device for lowering or raising a tripod head without changing the length of the tripod legs.

EMULSION—Gelatin or resin carrier of sensitized silver particles.

EMULSION SPEED—Reaction rate of different films to light.

ENLARGER—Photo-optical device to produce large pictures from small negatives.

ENLARGEMENT—Large print made from a smaller negative.

EXPOSURE—Activation of sensitive silver in the film by light. Admission of light into the camera through the lens.

EXPOSURE COUNTER—Numbering device for counting the exposures in the order that they are made.

EXPOSURE GUIDE—Chart suggesting aperture and shutter settings for differing conditions of light and subject.

EXPOSURE LATITUDE—Film ability to be over- or under-exposed and still yield an excellent picture.

EXPOSURE METER—Light intensity measuring device to indicate correct aperture and shutter settings.

EXTENSION FLASH—Coordinated multiple flash from different locations used to light a picture with greater balance.

FEATHERING—Using only the edge portions of a light in order to avoid a hot spot.

FILL-IN LIGHT—Diffused weak light usually used at the camera position to prevent too dark shadows.

FILTER—A colored glass that fits over lens and separates white light. May admit certain colors (transmission) while preventing other colors from coming through (absorption).

FILTER, GELATIN—Non-permanent filter usually used for experimental purposes.

FILTER, LAMINATED—Gelatin filter cemented between two pieces of glass.

FILTER, NEUTRAL DENSITY—Increases exposure without altering color values.

FILTER, POLARIZING—Transmits light rays of only certain angles. Minimizes glare.

FILTER, FACTOR—Additional exposure necessary because all filters retard some light.

FINE-GRAIN—Controlled small grain needed to produce negatives suitable for huge enlargements.

FIXING—Removing unexposed and undeveloped silver salts from an emulsion.

FIXED FOCUS—Standard camera distance scale setting with a narrow aperture which produces great depth of field and lessens the need for accurate focus. Box cameras are fixed focus.

FLASHGUN—Combined battery and flashlamp holder.

FLASHLAMP—Powerful single-use light source. Flash duration, generally 1/50 second.

FLASHTUBE—Powerful multiple-use light source. Flash duration 1/5000 second.

FLAT—Opposite of contrasty; showing little gradation of tone.

FOCAL LENGTH—The infinity (far distance) lens distance position from film.

FOCAL PLANE SHUTTER—Light admitting curtain similar to a window shade with a slit of varying size for different time intervals of exposure.

FOCUSING SCALE—Measurement chart which shows the required lens from film distance for different subject distances.

FOCAL FRAME—Convenient close-up camera device which eliminates the need for focusing or framing the subject.

GRAIN—Granular image breakdown due to optical or silver clumps formed by improper development.

GRADATION—Tone separation.

GLARE—Unwanted concentrations of light; hot spots.

GUIDE NUMBER—Flashlamp or flashtube reference number used to simplify the calculation of the proper aperture for different subject distances.

HI-LO SWITCH—Electrical device which permits focusing with dim lights and picture taking with brightened lights.

HARDENER—Toughens film or paper.

HOT SPOT—Undesirable concentration of light which over-exposes subject at the point of reflection.

HYPERFOCAL DISTANCE—Related focusing scale and aperture setting at which everything is in focus from half the set distance to infinity.

HYPO—Sodium thiosulfate, used to dissolve undeveloped emulsion on the film.

ILLUMINATION—Light necessary for photography. No illumination, no picture.

IRIS—Variable lens opening which may be adjusted to different sizes.

JIG—Holding device.

KELVIN (K°)—Visual comparison temperature number of a heated body.

LATITUDE—Permissible variation in exposure.

LEAF—One blade of a between-the-lens shutter.

LENS—Light-gathering system, usually of glass.

LENS CAP—Lens protective covering.

LENS HOOD, LENS SHADE—A light shield which prevents stray reflected light from entering the lens.

LENS SPEED, f/ NUMBER—Relationship of lens opening to film distance.

MASK—Shield; outline; cover.

MASK, BORDER—Uniform artistic outline around film or print.

MAIN LIGHT—Predominating light.

MERGER—Indistinct separation of subject or adjacent shades of color.

MICROFILMER—Convenient space-saving device for reproducing documents on 35mm film strips.

MIDGET LAMP ADAPTER—Device permitting the use of a small bayonet flashlamp in a standard size socket.

NEWTON RINGS—Irregular target-type spots resulting from imperfect mounting.

OVER-EXPOSURE—Too much light admitted for an exposure. Distorts tone values.

PANCHROMATIC—Black-and-white film sensitive to all colors.

PARALLAX—Viewpoint difference of camera lens and viewfinder.

PEAK-OF-ACTION—Apex, height of action.

PEAK-OF-FLASH—Broad plateau portion of the flashglow which makes flash synchronization possible.

PHOTO-ELECTRICITY—Electrical current generated when light strikes certain metals (selenium).

PHOTO-FLOODS—Incandescent lamps which burn brighter than normal because of over-voltage.

PHOTOMICROGRAPH—Picture taken by a camera through a microscope.

PLANAR—Single lens.

RANGEFINDER—Distance-measuring device, split-image or superimposed.

RANGEFINDER, COUPLED—Simultaneously measures the distance and correctly moves the lens focus into position.

READING—Estimate of an exposure by means of a photo-electric meter.

REFLECTOR—Device for directing light rays back to an area. Increases lamp efficiency.

REFLEX—Camera with image focused through a lens and reflected by a mirror onto a ground-glass.

RETAINING RING—Holding ring which keeps filter in filter adapter.

RETICULATION—Uneven wrinkling of the emulsion due to uneven temperature in development.

RETOUCHING—Pencil or brushwork on a negative or positive to improve the picture.

REVERSAL—Process which produces direct positives without a negative.

REWIND KNOB—Key or lever to wind film back into a cartridge.

SET-SCREW—Screw friction or mechanical device to limit the movement of mechanical parts.

SHORTSTOP—Solution which halts development.

SHUTTER—Device for governing the time interval that a lens remains open, like a water faucet that opens and closes.

SHUTTER RELEASE—Device for opening and closing a shutter.

SILHOUETTE—Subject is dark and outlined against the light background. Made by

over-exposing the background while under-exposing the foreground.

SINGLE-LENS REFLEX—Reflex which focuses by the same lens that takes the picture.

SLIDES—Mounted transparencies.

SOLENOID—Electro-magnetic shutter-tripping device used to synchronize flashlamps and flashtubes.

SPEEDLIGHT—An intense flash from a radio-type tube, 1/5000 second duration. Also called electronic or speed flash.

SPOTTING—Minimizing or obliterating scratches, spots, emulsion imperfections on the negative or positive.

SPOTLIGHT—Special type of point-source light which produces straight-line rays. Used for crispness, contrast, and sharp outline.

STOP—Opening; full 100% difference in light aperture; full opening of the iris number; from f/4 to f/5.6 is one stop.

STROBE—Speedlight.

SUPPLEMENTARY LENS—An additional lens placed over the regular camera lens used to alter focal length. Rigid cameras (non-bellows) usually use the positive type for close-ups.

SYNCHRONIZER—Mechanical or electrical device used to coordinate the opening of the shutter with the peak-of-flash.

TELEPHOTO LENS—Lens which produces an enlarged image as compared to the size produced with the regular lens, both pictures from the same camera position.

TEXTURE—Detail revealing; 90° angle of light for maximum effect.

TIMER—Measures hours, minutes, or seconds at regular intervals; may be audible when used for enlarging.

TIME EXPOSURE, T—Long exposure, requiring set-screw cable release or **T** setting on shutter.

TRIANGULATION—Subject distance measurement by observation from two points of view. Principle of rangefinder operation.

TRIPPING—Releasing the shutter.

TRIPOD—Sturdy, vibrationless camera support.

TRANSPARENCY—Film intended to be viewed by transmitted light.

TWIN-LENS REFLEX—Double camera type, with the top dummy camera used only for focusing.

UNDER-EXPOSURE—Insufficient light admitted for a good picture.

VALUE, COLOR—Relative brilliance (lighter or darker).

VIEWFINDER—Optical device to outline the subject area as seen by the lens.

VIGNETTE—Picture with a different border. Only the desired area is sharp.

WIDE-ANGLE LENS—Has a greater angle-of-view than the normal prime lens.

WINDING KNOB—Handle, lever, or key to move film forward to the next exposure.

Proxifocuser 35 for Argus C-3 (Photolix, Inc., Long Beach, N. Y.). Three models; focuses and corrects close-up parallax from 39" to 9".

CHAPTER 19 / **CLOSE-UPS AND PARALLAX CONTROL**

The viewfinder on your Argus miniature camera has been designed to frame your subject accurately at infinity and at most middle distances. As the camera is moved closer to the subject, you must reckon with the problem of parallax (difference of viewpoint of the camera lens and the viewfinder). If you do not correct for parallax in taking a portrait, your subject's head will be cut right through the forehead in the finished photograph. Other subjects will be poorly composed so that the resulting pictures will be in extremely poor proportion and generally not pleasing to the eye. With color work, exact framing is of paramount importance. Your subject must completely fill the negative area to get the maximum benefit of the film size. This must be done at taking time because cropping and enlarging are difficult with color film at present.

Because of the framing accuracy required with color, your viewfinder assumes a far greater importance at short distances. To help you correct for parallax, the parallax chart lists the dimensions for masking your viewfinder or combined rangefinder-viewfinder in the two parallax directions when the camera lens is both lower and displaced to either side of the taking camera lens. The correction from top to bottom is known as vertical parallax, while the correction from side to side is known as lateral parallax. After the viewfinder has been properly masked to correct for parallax, the exact subject-to-camera distance setting (focus) is the next item of importance. Close focusing with your Argus miniature cameras may be accomplished in these three ways:

1. Use a tape measure to determine the exact distance from the subject to the front of the supplementary lens which has been added over your prime camera lens. If a tape measure is not available, you can use a pre-measured string which is attached to the filter holder. The subject is brought to the end of the string. The string is allowed

48

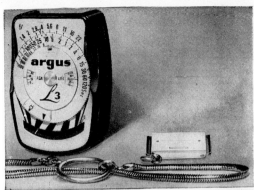

(above) The Argus Photo Exposure Meter. Readings of either incident light or reflected light are quickly and accurately made.

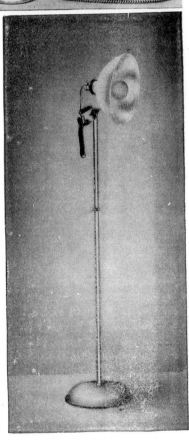

Elevating tripod

Floor Model

49

1   Regular lens only*

2   With Plus 1 Portra Lens*

3   With Plus 2*

4   With Plus 3*

5   With Plus 2 combined with Plus 3*

to fall out of the way, and as long as this pre-measured distance is maintained, you are in sharp focus.

Most regular lenses focus to three feet only. Focusing at shorter distances is possible with the use of an additional front supplementary lens (Portra-Lens Portrait, etc.). This added lens has a positive power and is fitted over your regular camera lens by means of a filter holder. This new Portra-Lens alters the point of focus of your regular lens so that very close subjects can now be brought into sharp focus. Supplementary lenses, depending on strength, may permit you to take pictures as close as three inches.

For a Safe-Set procedure, you can take a string and measure four distances (39 inches, 20 inches, 14 inches, 10 inches) and mark each one with a different colored tape. With a plus 1 lens, use the 39 inch setting and the 20 inch. The plus 2 can be used for the 20 and the 14. The plus 3 can be set with the 14 and 10. With these four settings and the f/11 iris stop you can cover most of your general needs.

2. A focal frame provides an easy method of determining the exact subject focus. It also frames your subject accurately at the same time. For certain forms of catalog work, using the focal frame is the best method of focusing because it can be built onto a regular light bar such as a Powell light. As long as all your short distance subjects are of the same size, the focal frame method permits a simple, rapid, routine, sure-fire technique that readily fits into the Safe-Set Method. The illustration shows a focal frame. It consists of a rigid outline of your field (10 percent larger to avoid its inclusion on the film) and the distance is fixed. With your subject distance and field size controlled accurately, the remaining problem of lighting and shutter speed may be similarly standardized. When the lights and shutter speed have been co-ordinated, you need merely add the correct Portra-Lens and then bring the outline up to the subject and release the shutter. Your picture will prove ideal because everything has been Safe-Set.

3. Near focusing optical devices which permit portraits to be taken with the C-3 and C-4 rangefinder cameras are being developed for use without a tape measure or a focal frame. Since they are optical devices, all parallax corrections are made simultaneously and within the camera. The Safe-Set Method for the use of these devices calls for pre-setting your near focusing distance after choosing the field size, and then moving the camera back and forth until the image in the rangefinder is complete. With a pre-set focus the slight focusing difference that may result is thoroughly compensated

Camera lens wide-open, shallow depth-of-field

Camera lens stopped down to increase the depth-of-field

Commercially available Reprox 12

Increase versatility of your C-3 with a set of three (5, 15, and 30mm) extension tubes for close-up focus from 3½ to 4 feet. (1:1 ratio). Photographic Import and Export Co.

by the large depth of field of your lens when it is set at the recommended f/11.

With regard to close-ups in general, keep in mind the following points:

1. With supplementary lenses (Portra-Lenses) your exposure is not changed by any factor.

2. Since the depth of field for any close distance is short, your lens-to-subject distance should be measured accurately.

3. Be certain that your body or camera does not shield the

MASKING FOR CLOSE-UP PARALLAX CONTROL

Camera		+1			+2			+3	
Mask in mm→	Top	Edge	Side	Top	Edge	Side	Top	Edge	Side
FA	1	--		2	--		3	--	
C3	1.5	1.5		2	2		3	3	
C4	1.4	1		2.5	2		3.75	3	

Focusing Scale		Lens to Subject Distance	Field Size Approximate	Depth of Field
+1	∞	38 3/4″	19″ x 28″	14″
	15	32 3/8″	16″ x 24″	9″
	4	21 5/8″	10″ x 15	4″
+2	∞	19 1/2″	9 3/8″ x 14″	3 1/2″
	15	17 3/4″	8 1/2″ x 12 3/4″	2 1/2″
	4	14″	6 1/2″ x 9 5/8″	1 5/8″
+3	∞	13″	6 1/4″ x 9 3/8″	1 5/8″
	15	12 1/4″	5 3/4″ x 8 3/4″	1 3/8″
	4	10 3/8″	4 3/4″ x 7 1/8″	1 3/8″

Parallax control mask

1. Place portrait lens in filter holder and place on lens.
2. Make mask of scotch tape or transparent film.
3. Place in view finder.
4. Focus and view the entire subject; then lift the camera so that subject is under the lower border of mask.
5. At the peak of composition or effect, release.
6. Wind and set for the next exposure.

Extension Tube Data for the C-3

Extension	Subject distance (front of lens)	Field in mm	Exposure Factors	Zone of Sharpness at f/11	Scale
5mm	25″	240x360	1.2	96	1:10
15	9″	80x120	1.5	11	1:3.4
20 (5 plus 15)	7″	60x90	2	6	1:2.4
30	5-2/3″	40x60	<.5	3.4	1:1.7
45 (30 plus 15)	5″	28x40	3.6	1.8	1:1.1
50 (30 plus 15 plus 5)	4″	24x36	4	1.4	1:1

light source from the subject. If this occurs, your pictures will be under-exposed.

4. Because of the relatively shallow depth of field, always pose your subject parallel to your camera. A subject with a great depth dimension cannot be completely maintained in sharp overall focus if he is placed at a 90-degree angle to the camera. But, by placing the same subject in a parallel plane to the camera body, a sharper focus will be assured.

A portrait is generally unappealing if it has an out-of-focus hand well in front of the subject. By turning your subject slightly to the side, this problem is either minimized or completely eliminated. These suggestions for focusing should help you solve this often vexing problem so that your entire picture area will be utilized, your subject will be in sharp focus and the actual picture-taking mechanics simplified.

CHAPTER 10 / FILM FOR BLACK-AND-WHITE PHOTOGRAPHY

Film consists of a layer of cellulose acetate, or other resin, acting as a base to support a complex gelatin emulsion composed of sensitized silver salts mixed with minute quantities of sensitive conditioning chemicals. Black-and-white film differs from color film in that the former generally has only one layer. While this one layer may be made sensitive to one or more colors at the same time, it is itself not color forming.

By the color response of black-and-white film, we mean the relative brightness in shades of gray that the film will show in recording the different colors of the spectrum, as compared to their true color visualization by the human eye. This is made clearer upon describing the three main black-and-white film types.

Panchromatic, Type B. Approximates the color sensitivity of the eye.

Blue sensitive. Activated fully only by blue light. Color blind to other true colors.

Infra-red. Sensitive to deep red and invisible red rays that the eye cannot see visually.

With this information you should be able to choose the right film for the right job. If you are copying newspapers, then only the blue-sensitive, fine grade positive film would be necessary. If you desire a mural from an outdoor architectural motif, then a fine grained (ASA25) or a micro-type emulsion (ASA8) would be the logical choice. For the beginner I suggest an ASA80 film such as Plus X because it combines speed, grain and color response.

As with any new field, you should first learn to use one film and one developer so that you may standardize your results for general picture taking. Later, you can use the special emulsions for the specific problems for which they were formulated. Here again, learn to use them under standardized conditions so that you may be always assured of a uniformity of result.

Tri-X film, produced by Eastman Kodak in the 35mm and 120 sizes, opens unexplored fields for regular black-and-white photography with existing light because of its very high emulsion speed. The film can be exposed at meter settings of A.S.A. 650 when developed in Microdol between 12 and 17 minutes, depending upon the contrast desired. The grain effect is similar to the older XX film. The amazing film speed allows pictures to be taken in normally lighted rooms at 1/30, f/3.5.

BLACK-AND-WHITE FILM

Film	Color Sensitivity	ASA D	T	Kodak Developer	Time Condenser	Diffuser	Use
Kodak Plus-X Supreme Superior 2	Pan B	50	40	D-76 Microdol Liquid/DK-20	11 12	13 14	All Around
Kodak Finopan, Superior 1	Pan B	25	20	D-76 Microdol Liquid/DK-20	9 10	11 12	Fine detail, contrast stereo
Kodak-XX; Superior 3; Ultra-Speed Pan	Pan B	100	80	D-76 Microdol Liquid/DK-20	13 15	15 17	Extra speed‡
Kodak Direct Positive	Pan B	64	50	Home Kit	—	--	One-step Slides; stereo
Bulk only Kodak Positive	Blue Sensitive	—	3		7	9	Black-and-White Copying
Kodak Micro-File Micropan, Minipan	Pan B	—	37	D-11	5 min.	6 min.	Finest grain
Kodak Infrared only with Kodak Wratten Filter No. 87 No. 25(A)	Infrared	—	4 3	D-76 Microdol Liquid or DK-20	9 10	11 12	

N.B. Pan B film with a Kodak Wratten Filter (2x) outdoors and a Kodak Wratten X-1 Filter (4x) indoors will duplicate in a gray scale the true color sensitivity of the eye.

CHAPTER 11 / **FILTERS FOR BLACK-AND-WHITE PHO-TOGRAPHY**

A filter may be defined as a separating or screening device which permits only specific colors or light rays to enter the camera lens while preventing undesired colors or rays from reaching the film. Filters for black-and-white photography serve many purposes when used with the many black-and-white film emulsions.

1. *Corrective.* Since an emulsion can only approximate the speed or color reaction of the human eye, there will always be a need to correct the response of the film so that it will approach the relative visual brightness through shades of gray that we see with our eyes. If we saw our world only in shades of white, black, and gray instead of colors, we would then be able to approximate the same tone scale as black-and-white film when it is activated by different colors.

2. *Contrast.* Another function of the filter is to distort color rendition of an emulsion for a dramatic or spectacular effect. Most night effects can be made during the day by the proper selection of filters. Contrasts may be accentuated to any end of the gray scale so that the tonal range may be either compressed or expanded.

3. *Polarization.* The polarization filter, because it transmits light vibrating only at a certain definite angle, helps to eliminate glare, purify colors, increase contrast and darken skies.

4. *Neutral density.* Many other emulsions are manufactured to a very high speed so that some means is required for certain taking phases, to actually reduce the amount of light entering the lens. If a filter is used to reduce the number of rays which enter the lens, it is necessary that it will maintain the correct color rendition of the subject. This is accomplished by using gray-toned filters which are graduated in density to reduce the amount of transmitted light without distorting colors or light values. They merely reduce the total amount of light entering the lens so as to permit a desired exposure when a very narrow opening is not possible, or a very high shutter speed cannot serve your purpose.

There are four filter types:

1. *Gelatin.* Where a large number of filters is needed for experimental work, gelatin filters are excellent because of their low price and easy adaptability. However, they require great care in handling because they show fingerprints and dust specks which are difficult to remove. Also the gelatin will frequently warp in a humid atmosphere if the filters are not stored properly.

2. *Cemented.* These filters are the most popular as they are inexpensive, function well, store easily, and can be kept clean because of the protective outer sides of glass.

3. *Dyed-in-the-mass glass.* These are the most durable filters, but careful selection is necessary to assure full color uniformity, duplication, and matching in sets.

4. *Water Cell.* This type of filter can be made by dissolving certain color chemicals in distilled water, and then placing the solution in a glass water cell. They may be used in front of hot lights so that the cell will function, in addition, as a heat-absorbing medium.

Coating filters with a thin layer of magnesium fluoride is a recent development. While coated filters are desirable, it is well to remember that many great pictures were taken before the advent of coated lenses. A coated filter, in itself, will not automatically produce a masterpiece. Great effort will always be required to create something that will be more than a snapshot.

With the exposure latitude of present day black-and-white film, the actual exposure with a filter over the lens is not too critical. You may overexpose or underexpose two stops either way and still get an excellent picture. Therefore, there is no need to compute each filter factor to precisely two or more decimal points.

Since a filter will admit only light of its own color, the color that is the same as the filter will be darker on the negative. Where the filter has excluded or rejected any color rays, the negative will be light, because no rays of this color enter the lens and expose the film. When this negative is printed, the heavy tones (the same color as the filter) will be light on the positive print, while the clear portion of the negative will print a dark gray or black, producing areas of shadow. From this information you can gather that to lighten a color you should use a filter of the same color while to darken the color you should use a filter which prevents any of the color to be darkened from reaching the film.

The chart in this chapter will give you all the required information to lighten or darken a subject's color by means of the appropriate filter.

It is important in making exposures to understand filter factors. Every piece of glass in front of your lens will absorb and prevent some light, however small, from reaching the emulsion. Since light is absorbed and excluded, you must compensate in some way for the rejected light that does not reach your emulsion, or your developed film will be underexposed. The additional exposure that must be given

Yellow filter effect (2x)*   Orange filter (3x)*

Green filter (4x)*   Red filter (8x)*

for each filter is known as the filter factor. You know that a red filter will hold back so much light that eight times the normal exposure must be given. A one-second exposure without a filter becomes an eight-second exposure with a red filter. Some technical filters have exposures of thirty times or more. You can see that unless adequate exposure compensation has been made for the additional light that is needed, forgetting a filter factor may ruin your picture.

Know the effect you want, and then use the proper filter to secure it. Do not over-filter, else the extra exposure will eliminate the desired tone or fine detail. Properly used, filters can become a valuable aid in interpreting your subject. "Shoot" a landscape with various filters, and you will be amazed how different the same scene can appear.

The Safe-Set Method for filter use is simple in that your filter factor is corrected on your emulsion speed setting of your exposure meter, chart, etc. So that if your filter factor is two, divide the emul-

BLACK-AND-WHITE FILTER INFORMATION
USE KODAK WRATTEN FILTER

The Subject Color	To Lighten a Color	To Darken a Color
VIB (violet,indigo,blue)	C-5	B
G (green)	B, G, or X-1	
Y (yellow)	K1, K2, G, or A	C-5
O (orange)	K1, K2, G, or A	C-5
R (red)	F, A, or G	C-5

FILTER FACTORS *for Panchromatic Emulsions, Type B*

Kodak Wratten Filter	Sunlight	T-Tungsten	Uses
K-2 (Yellow)	2	1 1/2	Produces normal skin tones, clouds (panchromatic film only)
G (Orange)	3	2	Darkens blues (sky tones, etc.), dramatizes outdoors
X-1 (Green)	4	3	Lightens foliage, separates different greens
A (Red)	8	4	(Panchromatic and Infra Red only) Blackens skies, night effects in daylight
Kodak POLA-SCREEN	4	4	Reduces glare, increases contrast, darkens skies.

N.B. Remember 2, 3, 4, 8 factor numbers for the standard black-and-white filters. Never over-filter.

Black-and-White Filters recommended for photography *cannot* be used with color film. Of the Filters included in the above table, only the Kodak Pola-Screen may be used with color film.

sion speed by two and use this new number on your calculator. In this way you will not have to be concerned with new calculations for each exposure. With the same filter in place, your exposure readings are made in a one-step direct procedure. In this way the pre-setting method reduces your chance of error and makes photography easy.

CHAPTER 12 / **PROCESSING FOR BLACK-AND-WHITE PHOTOGRAPHY**

After your film has been exposed, you must re-wind it back into the original cartridge or continue winding until the end of the paper backing can be pasted to prevent the film from unraveling. The exposed film appears no different from the unexposed film, but it is not capable of yielding an image. The potential undeveloped image is called by the scientists a "latent image." The changing of the invisible latent image to a visible permanent form is development.

Development must be performed entirely in the dark because your film is always sensitive to any light until the emulsion has been developed and completely fixed. It can be done either in a completely darkened room or with a light-tight development tank provided with an opening for changing the different solutions.

The amateur will generally find that darkroom development is a tedious process because so much of the time is spent in the dark just waiting. To make waiting more pleasant under normal light surroundings, the modern light-tight development tank has come into use. The film must be loaded in a darkroom. For an amateur, this may be a closet or a special type of changing bag. Once the film has been loaded into the tank, every other processing operation may be performed with full safety in daylight or roomlight. In using a tank be sure that your film is placed smoothly on the reel to prevent film buckling. For if this happens, an uneven white streak will appear on the positive print where the buckle has taken place.

There are two types of daylight development tanks available:

1. *Apron type.* Your film is wound around an apron that has raised dimpled studs at both edges. The studs separate the film from the apron and at the same time allow your developing fluids to circulate. This apron type often does not assure adequate fluid circulation because of the narrow space between film and apron. However, by turning the tank on its side and shaking continuously, this difficulty can be overcome.

2. *Reel type.* The reel type must be carefully loaded to prevent any buckling of the film. It is the more popular type of development tank in use. Here, too, your agitation should include shaking and turning the tank in addition to moving the reel by the core rod. Core rod agitation is not sufficient because the fluid at the center of the reel cannot escape. However, if you shake and turn the tank, the central column of fluid will be agitated and you will get complete circulation.

FILM FORMULARY

DEVELOPER	Elon (Metol)	Sodium Thiosulfate	Sodium Sulfite	Hydroquinone	Borax	Kodalk	Sodium Thiocyanate	Potassium Bromide	Sod. Carb. Mono.	Acetic Acid 28%	Chrome Alum	Boric Acid Crystal	Potassium Alum	Water to	REMARKS:
	Chemical - Grams														
DK-20	5.0		100			2.0	1.0	0.5						1000	Finest grain.
DK-20 R	7.5		100			20.0	5.0	1.0						1000	Replenisher - 1 oz. to a roll.
D-76	2.0		100	5.0	2.0									1000	Moderate grain.
D-76 R	3.0		100	7.5	20.0									1000	1 oz. to a roll.
D-76 F	2.0		100	5.0	20.0									1000	Existing light technique.
D-11	1.0		7.5	9.0				5.0	25.0					1000	High Contrast development.
SHORTSTOP 1.										120				1000	Neutralizes & stops development.
2.														1000	Water alone may be used.
3.											30			1000	Also hardens film.
FIXING BATH		240	15.0							48.0		7.5	15.0	1000	The ideal film fixer.
Diaversal Kit or First Dev.	1.5		25	5				2.0	50					1000	or Dektol 2:1 - Develop 1 min. - 60-68° F.
Second Dev.		5	50											+water to 24 ozs.	or Dektol 2:1+3.5 Gm.Hypo to 24 ozs. working sol.-Dev. 2 min.
														+First developer - 4 ozs.	
Toners 1. or	Eastman Rapid Selenium - 1 oz. to 32 ozs. water - Tone 1 to 3 minutes.														After toning, simply wash for 5 to 10 minutes. Roomlight may be turned on after first development.
2.	Ansco Flemish Toner - 1 oz. to 40 ozs. - Tone 1 to 3 minutes.														

Note: The beginner should purchase these formulae in a compounded, ready packaged, powder or liquid. Microdol Powder or Liquid replaces the packaged DK-20.

| Solutions will oxidize. | Inside floating paraffin lid in place. | Inside lid sinks as liquid is poured out. |

Once your film has been carefully loaded on to the film reel of your tank and the lid closed, you may then go into any light to start the development procedure. With black-and-white film, I would recommend that you do your own processing if you wish to bring out the full quality of the film. In addition to a developing tank, the other simple equipment for processing your own negative includes a thermometer and the developing solutions.

When you do not use these solutions for any length of time, the air affects them so that they lose their strength. When this happens, all your efforts as far as correct exposure, light control, etc. are concerned will be wasted. To minimize the possible spoilage through air oxidation, you can use the author's method for keeping your solutions fresh. Professionals use this device, the floating lid, to keep their solutions fresh for months at a time. The illustrations and directions below explain this easy method of protecting your processing solutions. Once you have made an inside floating lid for your bottles, you may be sure that your solutions will stay fresh for the maximum length of time, because your lid is a permanent addition. I would suggest that you prepare at least four or five bottles in this way so that you will have a couple of extra ones available at a moment's notice.

Materials: Paraffin (Parawax or any other brand of fruit preserve paraffin), bottles, water.

1. Fill your empty bottle with cold water up to where the shoulder starts to taper in.

2. Melt one half ounce (approximately ¼ bar) of paraffin in a double boiler, pot or heat proof glass dish. Melt carefully so that no open flame reaches the melting wax.

3. Pour the melted wax into the water-filled bottle. Let stand till completely cool. You will find that the wax has formed a thick layer on top of the water.

4. When you tilt the bottle the wax layer (floating lid) will move with the water. As you pour out water, the lid will sink to the lower water level.

5. Make up fresh processing solutions in properly labelled bottles with floating lids.

Make up at least four different floating lid bottles for:

(a) Developer, (b) Replenisher, (c) Chrome Alum Stop Bath, and (d) Fixer.

One question the amateur asks about developing is: Shall I mix my own formulae of individual chemicals, or should I purchase them ready for use? My advice would be to purchase your chemicals ready mixed. You will find that cheaper in the long run, because you are sure of the continued factory quality controls. With pre-weighed chemicals, all you have to do is dissolve the powder in the exact amount of water at a temperature the manufacturer recommends. Factory controls assure uniform quality, and the solutions will always be fresh and maintained at full strength if they are kept in the bottle with the floating lid described above. Should you, however, wish to mix your own chemicals, you will find two standard formulas listed in the table on page 62.

The second step in the development process is to rinse your film in order to halt film development. For this a stop bath of plain water, a solution of acetic acid (vinegar), or a solution of chrome alum may be used. The acetic acid solution can be used only once, while the chrome alum solution can be used again and again until a sediment forms. The chrome alum solution will also harden your emulsion so that reticulation (mottled film appearance) caused by uneven solution temperatures is kept to a minimum.

After the stop bath of chrome alum, another rinse with water is recommended to remove any chrome alum solution which may still be present on the film. After the water rinse has been poured out, the final step is to pour in your fixing solution. Fixing solution consists of a mixture of sodium or ammonium hypo-sulphite compound in water. This mixture has the property of moving only undeveloped silver salts. All that can remain in the emulsion is the developed (reduced) form of silver which is black or gray where the reflected light from your subject has reached the emulsion. Since the emulsion has thickness, the depth of the emulsion will be dark in direct proportion to the amount of light that has affected it. Little light causes little darkening; more light, proportionately greater darkening.

Only after the fixer has been in the daylight tank for approximately ten minutes do you open the tank to look at the film. If there is any cloudiness or murkiness to the emulsion, replace the film in the fixing solution for another five minutes. Remember that if your clearing time is over twenty minutes, it is a good idea to change your solution.

When your development has been completed, be sure to pour each solution back into its own bottle. Each bottle should be distinctly marked to prevent your contaminating solutions.

The best results are obtained with fresh processing solutions at a temperature of 68 degrees Fahrenheit (A.S.A.). It is axiomatic that the least expensive part of photography is the processing. Consider the fact that you spend a great deal of money and time taking pictures and then foolishly lose the value of this expenditure by trying to squeeze an extra roll from old, oxidized solutions. A small expenditure of money for fresh solutions will insure uniform results in development.

When the negative has been removed from the fixing solution it is washed in clear running water for at least ten minutes and then hung up to dry. Be sure that the negative is free from spots or water marks. To remove the sediment that sometimes adheres to film, wet a large wad of absorbent cotton, squeeze until it is damp, and then gently slide it along the negative to remove all surface sediment. Even the slightest amount of pressure must be avoided to prevent any chance of microscopic scratches being caused by the movement of the dampened cotton. These scratches, if formed, may show on enlargement and will require corrective treatment on the negative or print.

Great care in processing will produce its own reward—a perfect negative. Processing in photography is easy when you form the habit of doing it correctly. With correct processing, you will always know what uniform results may be expected. The good results which are attained by simpler standard methods will be satisfying and will spur you to greater efforts.

Color film is a miracle of this modern era of science. Since it consists of a filter layer combined with three sensitive emulsions, positioned one above the other, you are really taking three pictures. However, each emulsion layer reacts to only one of the primary colors. When the film is developed, the developing agents produce in each layer only the one specific color to which each emulsion layer is sensitive. When you view the film you see all three emulsions at one time. The eye combines the individual colors at this time so that you see all three pictures at once, forming in this way an impression of their true original color.

Contrasted with the many black-and-white film types, your color film is limited to two types—outdoor and indoor. It is very important to know that each color film must and can be used only for the light K° (Kelvin) to which it is balanced. By balancing the film for a particular light, we mean that the film's color rendition is adjusted for any particular K° of color such as daylight (5900°), photofloods (3400°), or commercial 3200-degree Tungsten lamps. The amateur generally will use the popular, available photofloods (3400-degrees K). These balance so perfectly with Kodachrome Type A that no filter is necessary.

The degrees K represents a scientific light temperature reference point for measuring, describing, and comparing any light source with the color quality of a heated black body (iron). As iron is heated, it slowly turns different colors through a deep red, cherry red, orange, yellow, blue, and blue-white as it gets progressively hotter.

The chart shows the different color films that are available and other pertinent information. It is thrilling to know that color film materials are in a state of day-to-day evolution. The latest individual methods for color processing may be found on the excellent information sheet which accompanies every roll of color film. Eastman Kodak is the company which processes Kodachrome; Ansco Color may be processed locally or may be sent to any official processing laboratory. The occasional user would be wise to permit only a regular color finishing laboratory, which has the necessary delicate control equipment, to develop his film. Remember that color film processing requires a great deal of care and allow only those who specialize in such matters to handle your color processing work.

COLOR FILM

Film Name	Color Balance	A.S.A. Setting	Conversion Filter	New A.S.A.	New Balance	Processing
Kodachrome Daylight	6500°	10	-	-	-	Local and Kodak
Kodachrome F	Flash 3800°	-	82A 85C	10 10	Flood-3400°K Daylight	Local and Kodak
Ektachrome Daylight	6500°	32	-	-	-	Local, Kodak and home kit
Ektachrome F	Flash 3800°	-	82A 85C	16 20	Flood-3400°K Daylight	Local, Kodak and home kit
Ansco Color Tungsten	Flood 3400°	12	#11	10	Daylight	Local, Ansco and home kit
Anscochrome Daylight	6500°	32	-	-	-	Local, Ansco and home kit

N.B. Kodachrome, at this writing, possess the finest grain and best saturation of colors.

Ansco Color may be bought in bulk and spooled in individual cartridges. Always remember to color balance your color film. Remember also to keep your ratio of highlight volume to shadow volume within the narrow latitude inherent in reversal color positives, never higher than 4 to 1.

The amateur will find that the best bet is to use indoor Kodachrome Type A. With Type A, the film problem is simplified so that you can use inexpensive photofloods or SM-SF flash indoors without any filter, while outdoors you can use color conversion #85 filters. With these conversion filters, one film may be used both outdoors and indoors with greatest film-speed efficiency. Use the filters outdoors only; they are not needed indoors. Type A film used outdoors gives you the additional advantage of clearing distant haze which gives a warm, pleasing effect to your pictures.

67

Color film requires an entirely different type of filter than black-and-white. Therefore, never use any of the black-and-white filters, with the exception of the polarizing neutral filter, for color work.

As we have mentioned before, the all-important problem with color film is color balance. Color balance is the attempt to bring the color temperature of your lights to match the color film's adjustment. You will find that with this color matching, you are right back with our old friend Kelvin°.

If your color film is balanced for 3400 degrees Kelvin (photofloods) and you use incandescent lamps, which produce only 3200 degrees Kelvin, then you'll find that your finished transparencies will be too warm (reddish) in color. If you have only 3200° lamps to take these pictures, you must compensate with special correcting filters. These special filters are placed over the camera lens and you'll find that the light balancing filters (LB for short) will raise or lower the color temperature of your light source to that required by the film so that you will be able to produce a temperature-balanced color transparency.

Do not be a filter collector. You may use daylight film outdoors in order to avoid using any filters. Therefore, use indoor Kodachrome (A) with photofloods and Ansco Color (3200°) with its specific lamps. Slight differences of color temperature can be tolerated by the eye without any fretful worry of super-scientific measurement with a color meter. The proof is the millions of acceptable transparencies which have been made by novices who have never heard the term "Kelvin degrees."

COLOR FLASH

The critical color temperature of your film requires that you use a light balancing filter (81C) when using photoflood (3400°) or (81D) incandescent (3200°) film with flashlamps (3800°). Because flashlamps burn at a 3800-degree Kelvin temperature, it is necessary to bring the K° down to the 3400-degree or 3200-degree Kelvin temperature with a light balancing filter as the chart shows. With an SM-SF lamp, no filter is required as the color

FILTER DATA FOR KODAK COLOR FILMS			
Lighting Conditions	Daylight Type	3400° Type A	Ektachrome F
Daylight, Clear or hazy sun casting Sharp or soft shadows	No Filter required (See Note 1)	Daylight Filter for Type A Kodak Color Films (No. 85)	Daylight Filter for Type C Kodak Color Films (No. 85C)
Daylight, Bluish-open shade or overcast. No shadows	Skylight (No. 1A)	No. 85	No. 85C
Daylight, Distant scenes, mountain & aerial photography	Skylight (No. 1A)	No. 85	No. 85C
Electronic Flash Tubes	Kodachrome: None Ektachrome: CC-10Y (see film instructions)	Not recommended	Not recommended
Blue Flash Lamps	No Filter Required	Not recommended	Not recommended
Daylight Fluorescent Lamps	Kodachrome: CC-20B Ektachrome: CC-10M + CC-05B	Not recommended	Not recommended
Blue Photoflood Lamps	Not recommended	Not recommended	Not recommended
Photoflood Lamps	Photoflood Filter for Daylight Type Kodak Color Films (No.80A)	No Filter Required	No. 82A
3200 K Lamps	No. 80A + No. 82A	No. 82A	No. 82B
Flash Lamps No. 5, 6, 11, 22, 31 & 50	Not recommended	No. 81C	No Filter Needed
Flash Lamps No. 0, 2, 2A, 3, 25, 26 & 40	Not recommended	No. 81D	No Filter Required
SM Flash Lamps	Not recommended	No Filter Needed	No. 82B
SF Flash Lamps	Not recommended	No. 81A	No. 82B
Standard Warm White Fluorescent Lamps	Not recommended	CC-10Y + CC-20M	No Filter Needed
Standard Cool White	Not recommended	CC-40Y + CC-30M	No Filter Needed

*Not available in miniature camera size.

HOME PROCESSING EKTACHROME 35mm			
Film	Color Balance	A.S.A.	With Conversion Filters
Ektachrome E	Daylight	32	---
Ektachrome F	#5, 25, 6, 26FP, 11, 0, 2, 22 Not SM, SF, or M-2	-	85C Daylight 20 82A Photoflood 16

temperatures of these lamps approach that of Type A to within a reasonable degree. The slight difference of color temperature may produce light ruddy tones which enhance the color quality. You will find that this color correction information ought to be carried with you at all times. It is sad, indeed, to have an otherwise perfect picture spoiled just because of improper color balance. In a later chapter you will be shown for the first time how you can correct poor color slides. But it is far more important that you do the right thing at the beginning and "have it on the negative."

COLOR LIGHT BALANCING AND CONVERSION FILTERS

Ansco Color Light Balancing Filters (courtesy Ansco Company)

UV-15   1.   Haze correction (slight)

        2.   For photoflood correction with Ansco Color, Tungsten Type.

UV-16   1.   Haze correction (medium)

        2.   For clear flash lamp correction with Ansco Color, Tungsten Type.

        3.   In enlarger's optical system, in addition to recommended filters when exposing Ansco Color Printon.

UV-17   1.   Haze correction (strong).

      #10   Conversion For 3200° correction with Ansco Color, Daylight type (4x).

      #11   Conversion For daylight correction with Ansco Color, Tungsten type ($1\frac{1}{2}$x).

      #12   Conversion High-Speed strobe correction with Ansco Color, Tungsten, type.

KODAK COLOR LIGHT BALANCING FILTERS (courtesy Eastman Kodak Company).

BLUISH FILTERS	EXPOSURE INCREASE IN STOPS*	YELLOWISH FILTERS	EXPOSURE INCREASE IN STOPS*	YELLOWISH FILTERS	EXPOSURE INCREASE IN STOPS*
No. 82 (CC3)	1/3	No. 81 (CC13)	1/3	No. 81E	2/3
No. 82A (CC4)	1/3	No. 81A (CC14)	1/3	No. 81F	2/3
No. 82B (CC5)	2/3	No. 81B (CC15)	1/3	No. 81G	1
No. 82C (CC6)	2/3	No. 81C	1/3	No. 81H	1
		No. 81D	2/3		

*These values are approximate. For critical work, they should be checked by practical tests, especially if more than one filter is used.

TEMPERATURES (K°) OF COMMON LIGHT SOURCES.

1300°	Candle flame
2200°	Drying, heat, red ray lamps
2400-3100°	Home incandescent light lamps
3200°	Commercial photographic color lamps
3300°	SM-SF flash lamps
3350°	CP lamps for color photography
3400°	Photofloods
3500°	White fluorescents or sun, one hour after sunrise
3300°	Regular photoflash
4400°	Sun, two hours after sunrise
4500°	Bright-white fluorescents
4800°	Blue daylight photofloods
5800°	Average noon-day sun
6000°	Blue (daylight) photoflash
6500°	Strobe, electronic flash
7000°	Uniform overcast sky
10,000°	Blue sky
20,000°	North blue sky

CHAPTER 15 / **L—LIGHT SOURCES**

The first and most important subject that will greet you at the doorway to photographic knowledge will be light. Only when your subjects reflect light can they be photographed. Recording of this reflected light may take place only by means of light-sensitive film. If there is no subject to reflect light, then no matter how long your exposure may be there can be no picture. Similarly, unless you have a light-sensitive emulsion to record the effects of light, there can be no picture. The two essential elements for a picture are an emulsion that is light-sensitive and light.

We have discussed various types of film and film characteristics. We will now detail the preparation, use, and the effects of different kinds of lignt.

There are three basic light types as shown in the chart. The photographic effects of these different types should serve as a guide for their use with various subjects.

You can choose the proper type of light for any subject. An old wrinkled woman should not be photographed with the same light type you would use with a weather-beaten character. To soften the wrinkles of Granny and so make her love you all the more for making her look younger, you ought to use either heavily diffused photofloods, bounce light, or fluorescents if they are available. The weather-beaten realism of your battered character whom you wish to portray in vivid dramatic contrast can be brought out only by using the spotlight at the proper angle, or using outdoor sunlight as a point source of light.

If you wish to reveal the fine texture of a lace pattern, then a properly angled spotlight will be the logical choice to show all the crisp detail. On the other hand, if you wish to minimize the detail in order to get an area effect for mood, then a diffused source is the choice for the desired result.

It is necessary to emphasize that while a sharp contrasting light may be diffused, one can never sharpen the effect of a diffused light source. For this reason many photographers always use spotlights and then soften their image while enlarging. This technique is applicable only to black and white film since there is no possibility of changing your lighting effect with color film.

72

Spotlight (point source)

Floodlights (semi-diffused)

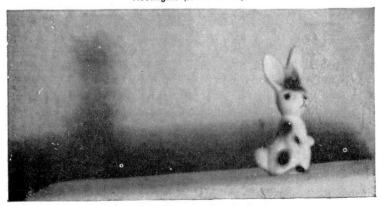

Fluorescent (diffused)

1. The *point* source of light produces rays which travel in a perfectly straight line. Since the light direction is straight, any shadow that is cast will be sharp. Only a point source of light can produce a sharp shadow. The full shadow effects are:

a. Sharp
b. Crisp
c. Contrasting
d. Penetrating

N. B. A point source of light may have its rays directed into a small area by use of a Fesnel-type condensing lens which avoids "hot spots."

2. A *semi-diffused* light is the most popular type of light source used (photofloods, frosted incandescents). The reasons for their popularity are:

a. Inexpensive
b. Available anywhere for the amateur
c. Provide sufficient light for short exposures
d. Have the correct color temperatures for color film
e. Available with built-in reflectors (RFL-2).
f. Commercial bar equipment available to hold a large number of floods for portability and convenience.

3. A *diffused* (scattered) light type has its rays completely scattered, at the source, in all directions. The illustrations show that the shadow forms produced by (1), (2) and (3). The diffused type shadow is completely formless.

Since there is no definite shadow cast with this type of light it is an ideal choice when one wishes to minimize detail or avoid shadows. The newest type of diffused (scattered) light is called an "area fluorescent." The light-emitting phosfors are impregnated in a flat, small tile form. The tile may be placed or built into any pattern anywhere. This offers promise for use as an evenly balanced room or studio over-all illumination source or fill-in depending upon how you build up your I-G-A-S formula. (See page 85.)

Expensive equipment is not necessary. With the intelligent use of a few floodlamps, you can produce as great a variety of pictures as anyone would ever wish. The angle of coverage for your floodlamp is adequate for most amateur indoor or outdoor subjects. The only advantage of commercial equipment lies in the even coverage of very large areas. Your efforts, with either amateur or commercial equipment, will be excellent if you know the effect that you want—and take the care to produce it.

DIFFERENT TYPES OF LIGHT

TYPE	INDOORS	OUTDOORS	SHADOW	CONTRAST	SUBJECTS
(1) Point SMALL (IDEAL)	Carbon arc Zirconium	Clear, sunny day	Sharpest	Steep	Emphasize texture
LARGE	Incandescent Spotlight Flashlamp Flashtube Bare clear Tungsten Lamp Clear floods				Male portraits Medical detail Accentuation stage Commercial
SHAFT	Ring flashtube				

A mirror will retain the character of the light type

A matte or semi-matte reflector (aluminum, whiteboard, etc.) produces a mixed quality light source.

TYPE	INDOORS	OUTDOORS	SHADOW	CONTRAST	SUBJECTS
(2) Semi-diffused (MOST USED)	Diffusing media over any point light source Frosted incandescent Frosted floods Aluminum reflectors	Hazy sun	Outline hardly distinguishable	Moderate	Main light, Most amateur still or movie portraits
(3) Diffused SCATTERED	Line fluorescents Cold cathode Circline Area lighting Bounce light Matte board reflectors White wall Open book or newspaper White towel, etc. Thick diffusion of (1) and (2)	Cloudy, dull day	Very fuzzy	Little	Fill-in "soft" general illumination minimum subject and detail contrast

CHAPTER 16 / **A—ANGLE ARRANGEMENT**

You will shortly find that the arrangement and placement of your lights is a very important factor to be considered. The illustrations demonstrate the results of different light positions, while the chart details the effects for which each different position may be used.

Once again you can choose the best light position for any particular effect. At the beginning you will consult the chart for its recommendations, but as you progress you will automatically place the lamps in their correct position without even thinking twice as to what is being done. With experience, you will know what has to be done and will do it!

ANGLE DIRECTION OF LIGHT

Angle of Light	Use	Type
0° Front light	Fill-in. Must not cast a shadow	Semi-diffused or diffused
45° on each side	Flat copying	Any
45° subject to camera and 45° from front down. (Classic Portrait Light)	Main Illumination	Point for men Semi-diffused for most Diffused for subduing detail
45° Front rear down on subject	Accentuation	Spotlight
45° up on near wall, etc.	Separation	Floodlight in bullet reflector
90°	Texture Maximum detail contrast	Any depending upon vigor of detail required
38°	Limit eyeglass reflection	Any
180°	Rim effect — full subject Halo effect	Bare lamp without reflector behind subject; controlled spotlight on background
33½° Polarizer	Reduce glare and reflection Increase contrast Increase color purity Eliminate haze (outdoors)	Any

76

In the following eight panels, page 78, one can see the effect of light upon a model, in each case the lamps being placed at floor level and at intervals of 45 degrees in a complete circle about her. Lighting from low angles is mostly used to create dramatic effects of suspense or grotesqueness. It is often seen in shots of wrestlers, boxers, fortune tellers.

In the chart of photos (9–16) page 79, 8 flashbulbs were positioned at camera level encircling the model. Notice the visible differences in the lighting when compared with the matching panels: 9 and 1, 11 and 3, and so on. By studying these areas of illumination in the four charts you can formulate lighting combinations to fit your own lens subjects.

Photos 17–24, page 80, show what happens when lights are raised to an angle of 45 degrees above, and directed upon, a subject. Number 18 is the classic 45/45 main light position. Wide side, back and top light positions shield lamp and lens to avoid flare. These charts are useful to determine flash fill-in angles for outdoor shooting as well as indoor work.

Lamps at an angle of 70 degrees above the model's head give the results seen in photos 25–32, page 81, with number 33 being a direct, overhead top light. In the main, these positions are used for highlight accents in so-called glamour shots. In setting up lights keep in mind these 33 basic illumination effects and use combinations which best suit the subject.

Photos on pages 78, 79, 80, 81, *by Ed Hannigan for Sylvania Electric from U. S. Camera*

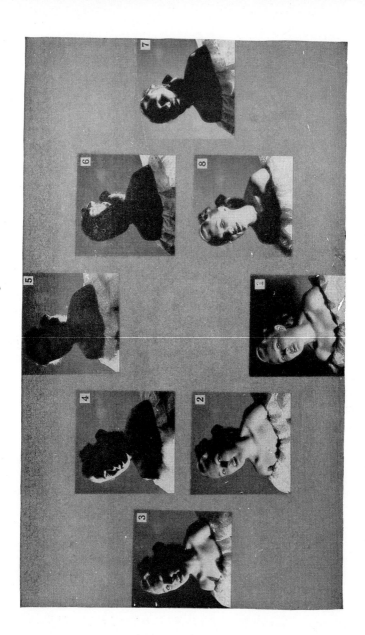

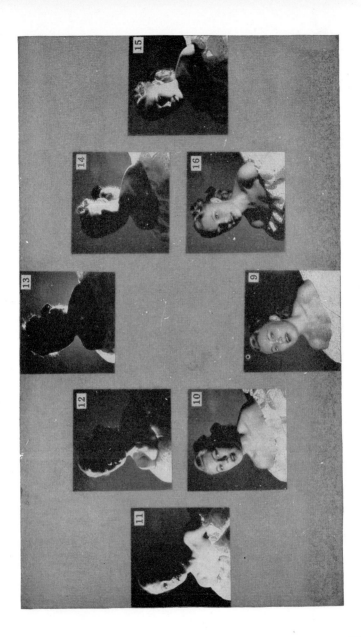

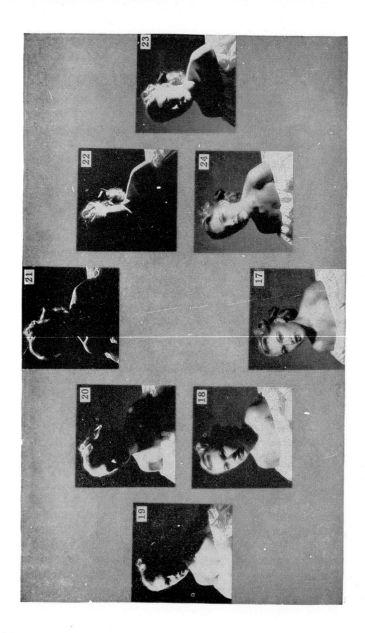

80

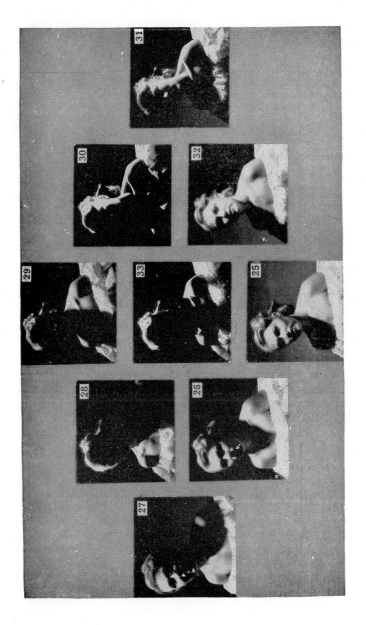

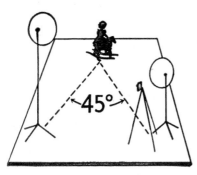

Diagram for light placement and balance.*

Simple baby picture*

Basic Side **Basic Front** **Back-light** **Accent-light**

A	**B**

Both A and B are lighted with a Basic Side and a Basic Front light.
In addition A has a Back light while B has an added Accent light

The most important characteristic of film, you will discover, is that the emulsion does not have the same sensitivity to differences in light strength as does the human eye. On a bright day, you can see and distinguish light differences up to 2000 to 1. For practical purposes, a photographic film can distinguish a volume ratio of only 60 to 1. This usual ratio of 60 to 1 serves admirably for most black-and-white film. For color film, this ratio sensitivity is further compressed to approximately 4 to 1 maximum. Do not be discouraged because of this seemingly low contrast value. Millions of photographs have been made within these contrast limitations and their results have been entirely satisfactory. Since the sensitivity latitude of your film must have the volume ratios of light in the proportions that we have indicated, you must light your subject so that the volume ratios are within the confines of the specific latitude limits. The illustrations demonstrate what occurs when you use the ratios of the light within the film latitude permitted. At 16 to 1, there is just a trace of shadow detail. The shadow detail increases as you increase the proportion of light onto the shadow side. At 1 to 1, both sides are equally lit. To simplify this balancing of light within the confines of the film capacity to record shadow, middle-tone and highlight volume, the author has coined the IGAS formula. (*I*-Illumination; *G*-Gradation; *A*-Accentuation, *S*-Separation.) This formula serves as the basis for all exposure balance in photography. It must be used for all photography. The type, the angle, the quality of light may change, but unless the light volume is kept within the proportions of the IGAS formula, there will be no picture.

I—Illumination. We have established that light is essential for any photograph. In order to build up your lighting for your subject, you must start out with a main source of light. The main source of light—point, semi-diffused or diffused depending on the wanted effect—acts as an overall light source, and should illuminate the entire subject. This light source serves as the reference point for calculating all the ratios before determining your exposure. The position for this main light is generally at a 45-degree angle. This means that the light should shine onto the subject from a 45-degree angular height and be placed at a 45-degree angle in relationship of the subject to camera lens. If you use a human figure as a model and shine your main source of illumination onto the figure at the

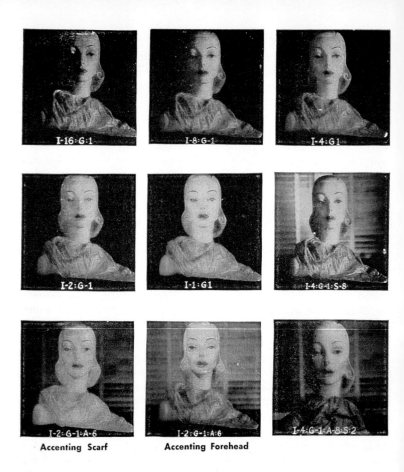

I-16:G:1   I-8:G-1   I-4:G1

I-2:G-1   I-1:G1   I-4:G-1:S-8

I-2:G-1:A-6   I-2:G-1:A:6   I-4:G-1-A-8-S:2

Accenting Scarf   **Accenting Forehead**

angles described, you will find that direction of light will cause shadow on those portions of the figure which are not directly facing the light. While your eyes, because of their great contrast range, can see the details on the shadow side of the subject, you now know that the shadow side will be recorded by your film as murky splotches or dark spots. In order to bring details into the shadow side of your subject so that there will be gradation within the shadow spots, you know that you must bring additional light onto these areas. In order to raise the ratio of light to dark so that it is at least within the minimum sensitivity of light to dark range of 60 to 1, you must study the next light—the G-light.

84

G—Gradation. The shadow side of your subject must receive more light. The fill-in, or balance, light may be provided by two means. You can reflect your illumination light back into the shadow portion of your subject by means of a white sheet, an open book, newspaper, or by posing your subject next to a wall. For easier control, another lamp may be used. The light strength of this lamp is generally weaker than your main source, or *I*-light. The *G*-light is most often placed right next to the camera, so that there is an even fill-in of your light. You must be careful to see that the *G*-light is thoroughly diffused. If it is not, it will produce shadows of its own. The multiplicity of shadow is annoying to look at and will show you that there is proper lack of light control. You may use a large lamp as strong as your main light for a fill-in, but the placement distance must be much further away. Light varies geometrically to the subject distance. This means that if at two feet your light delivers one unit of light, at four feet it will deliver only one-quarter of the amount of light. While the lights may appear pretty close together to your eye, you should accurately measure distances in order to assure yourself of proper light valuation. Your subject will now be properly illuminated for picture-taking, and you will find that, as with all things, there must be one point of interest. This point of interest must be emphasized. Here is how it is done.

A—Accentuation. To accentuate your subject, it is necessary that you provide a crisp, concentrated, powerful light source that can be easily controlled within a very limited area. Spotlights are manufactured with accessory masks and lenses which permit varied sizes and shapes of light to be placed in any small area that you may desire to accentuate. By now, you know that film has its characteristic limitations. In order to accentuate any portion of your subject, you must bring more light onto that area. If you calculate your overall exposure for your accentuation light, then everything else will be in shadow. Therefore, leave your exposure as it was with your *I*-light, but strengthen your accentuation light in the over-proportion of 2 or 3 to 1 times that of your illumination light. This will assure that your main subject will be produced in thoroughly exposed and developed middle tones and shadows, while the spotlight will delineate the accentuation point so that it will be exposed and developed in the highlight portions of your film. Since the eye always travels to the lighter portion of the picture, you will have provided the point of accentuation which you have desired. You will have been able to delineate and highlight your subject so that it will have good tone gradation with an interesting point of interest. You will find that your subject matter is necessarily a part of a scene. If you leave your lighting as you have calculated up to now, your subject will photograph merged against a wall or area which will be black or dark. The hair of your subject will merge with the dark shadows so that the improper background will be disturbing and artistically undesirable.

S—Separation. In order to get the subject placed without a merger, it is necesary that you light your background so that it will be truly distinct as part of the subject scene. Another purpose of the separation light is to separate your subject from the surrounding medium. This can be done in a number of ways, all of which depend upon the basic fact that the film sensitivity requires a definite light volume balance so that the film can adequately record light and dark.

If you use a white wall and do not permit any light to fall on it, the wall will photograph black. If 1/16 the amount of the main light reaches the wall, the wall tone will get lighter, If the ratio of light reaching the white wall is within 3 or 4 to 1, the wall will photograph gray. If the light ration reaches 1 to 1, the white wall only now will photograph white. A light is generally placed upon the floor and shone upon the wall within the ratios desired, so that your subject will be separated from the wall. If you place your subject in front of a window you can control the amount of light entering the room by using a Venetian blind which is gradually closed until the proper ratio is reached; outdoors you may use reflectors, using reflected skylight to lighten wall shadows. In color photography, the exposure ratio has an additional factor —that of suitable color contrast. This can be gotten by consulting a color wheel.

Light: Inverse Square Law

It is important to understand the rules governing the distance of your light from your subject. It is far more serious to move a light from two feet to four feet than from 10 feet to 12 feet although in both cases the light is moved two feet.

1. When your light is moved from 2 feet to 4 feet, the light-to-subject distance is halved. At half the distance, the exposure is $\frac{1}{4}$ the amount. If your exposure was one second

with the light at 2 feet, it will be 4 seconds with the light at 4 feet.

2. When your light is moved from 10 feet to 12 feet, the difference is only 20% and your exposure factor would be 1½ times or 1 second at 10 feet and 1½ seconds at 12 feet.

3. Although the different light movement has been 2 feet in both examples, in the closer distance, the exposure factor is 4 times; with the further distance the factor is only 1½ times.

4. Take great care in measuring your lights at very close distances because of significant exposure differences that occur even with relatively small movements.

5. Color film requires precise measurement to the point where a ruler must be used for flash-to-subject measurement to insure proper exposure.

6. If you cannot move your lights, then place one clean white handkerchief over the lamp to reduce by ½ the available light, 2 handkerchiefs for ¼, and 3 handkerchiefs for ⅛ light output reduction. This knowledge is important for outdoor flash fill-in. Since, in most cases, you cannot remove the flash from the camera, you may use as many handkerchief layers as is necessary to reduce the flashlamp's light until it balances with your sunlight ratio.

The popularity of 35mm color film has brought the request for more color information. You must realize that no matter how many books are written about color, the basic factors to be considered are the narrow limitations of the photographic emulsion to record light ratios only up to a 4 to 1 volume. The determination of what colors to use is covered in Chapter 25. That chapter will show you how to calculate your color contrasts so that you will be able to get the maximum effect.

As color film is very expensive, you will want correctly exposed pictures every time. The care and consideration that you take in lighting your films will be rewarded with better pictures and fewer failures. When you take preliminary care in your light ratio photography, you can be sure of a high percentage of successful pictures. Once you understand how to light a picture, you will be delighted by the countless variations which are possible. By altering the angle, the type or quantity of light, for the *I*, the *G*, the *A* and *S*, you will be able to easily change the meaning of the picture. This control lifts photography from a mechanical science to an art. You will develop your own technique and your own preferences; you will no longer be dependent upon any set of lights or a camera. You will discover that there are two types of people. One person will try to specifically duplicate a camera, shutter speed, openings and lights to the inch. His efforts will be rewarded with just a duplicating effect. The other person will know what to do and will so arrange any light, any camera, any subject with the teachings of the Universal LABS formula that his efforts because of his flexibility will produce something greater than a photograph—a picture.

CHAPTER 18 / S—SUBJECT COMPOSITION

The L-A-B portions of the Universal Formula have taken care of your film, type of light-source, light angle placement, balance of lights, and even the correct exposure, yet you will still not get a worthy picture if your subject is not suitably arranged.

Numerous books have been written, and numerous books will be written as to what constitutes a pleasing picture. For simplicity's sake, whatever pleases you is, for you, the most satisfactory picture. There are rules of composition, but like all rules they are broken and need to be broken for effect. You will find that if all your compositions are always made exactly to the rules, the pictures, after a time, will be stilted and stale. However, the standard rules of composition should serve as a base.

There is such a thing as style in a photograph. If you have studied photographs of the acknowledged masters, you can spot their work without any difficulty as they have a characteristic style, approach, and finish to their pictures. These different characteristics were not acquired in one day. In fact, at this point, it is helpful to mention that as an amateur, you may take one or two rolls of film and find that perhaps only one or two frames will meet your requirements. Do not be discouraged, for the same thing occurs with professionals. You naturally assume that the published work of the professional is the best. It is the best, but of very many exposures. A group of 30 or 40 pictures may produce 2 or 3 which exactly meet their needs. If this is the case, you can take heart in realizing that photography, while being simple in mechanical nature, still requires a combination of judgment and skill.

View your picture at intervals for a week, and you'll learn just how good it is by living with the picture. A simple rule of composition is to divide your viewfinder into thirds both vertically and horizontally. Place your center of interest (the main reason for a picture) at the intersection of any two lines. Since very fine lines are difficult to draw, you may place four pin-point dots drawn by a fine crow quill pen with India ink. If you place your main interest at a dot, you will find that your subject composition immediately become dynamic (active) rather that static (monotonous). With color, it is very important to mention that you can not change your composition after the picture is taken by means of enlarging, cropping, etc. Therefore in composing for color, your composition must be "tight." There must be no waste of film area, else your produced image will be far too small for adequate projection. Your composition may be built on the principle of a geometric form such as:

1. Circle, semi-circle, concentric rings.
2. Squares of different sizes.
3. S-curve.
4. Triangle or pyramid.
5. Cross.
6. L-shaped motif.
7. Uneven numbered similar patterns.
8. Diagonals.
9. Converging or diverging lines.

No matter which motif (form) is used, your subject must, as we have mentioned before, always have a center of interest. Your ability to place the center of interest in an appropriate surrounding is the measurement of your ability to produce fine compositions. While many people have an innate sense of composition, the mechanical choice of form may be taught and mastered.

Color introduces an additional factor because of the need for color harmony. The chapter on color will guide you to choose the classically correct colors.

When you have chosen the proper type of light, arranged

the angles of your lights, balanced your light volumes to your film latitude, and correctly composed your subject, the only remaining item is to "click your shutter." The result sometimes will be a photograph. But, at intervals, you will amalgamate your technical and subjective factors into a welded unit of creation which will yield a masterful picture.

ANALYSIS CHART

1. Camera & Lens	2. Film & #	3. Illumination	4. Angle	5. Gradation	6. Angle	7. Accentuation	8. Angle	9. Separation	10. Angle	11. Filter	12. Exposure	13. Negative Development Time	14. Paper & Grade	15. Paper Developer	16. Remarks
	PX	#2F	45°	#1F	camera	spot	one	#2F	45°	K-2	f/8	D-76	VanGam	D-72	
	#1	H	45°	1	height	8	hair	2	up		1/25	14	#5		
	#2														
	#3														
	#4 etc.														

Using the Analysis Chart: List only factors that are important.

1. List the camera and lens.
2. Name of Film and the number of the exposure.
3. In the Illumination box, top half names the lamp used, the bottom half the ratio of light balance.
4. Record the angles of your light to the subject.
5. Gradation box: top half for the lamp used, bottom half for the ratio of light balance.
6. Angles of the Gradation light.
7. Accentuation: top half for the lamp, bottom half for the light ratio.
8. Angles of Accentuation light.
9. Separation light: top half for the lamp, bottom half for the light ratio.
10. Angles of the Separation light.
11. Filter
12. Exposure used, etc.

The analysis chart is a positive record of what you did for your exposure. The final print will show wherein any faults may be. From this information you can improve your pictures. Use it!

CHAPTER 20

ARGUS EXISTING-LIGHT (10X) PHOTOGRAPHY

THE TREND TO NATURALNESS

The effects of direct, bounce, and existing-light photography are characteristically different. Only existing-light or prevailing light photography retains the original mood and effect. Since it uses the normal existing light, it avoids the use of flashlamps, flashtubes, or other disturbing elements which may break the cooperative mood between photographer and subject. However, modern existing-light photography, to be successful, requires special attention to the processes of taking, developing, and printing. Its unique effects will be obtainable if you follow the directions step by step.

DEFINITION

The existing light level is generally low. As the name implies this is the only light you will be using—that is, normal illumination not designed for photography. It may be the sole spotlight on a stage, the regular room light, or even a dimly lighted wall fixture, etc. The light level is usually so low that normal procedures might seriously underexpose the picture. To compensate for this absence of light we can modify our developing technique. This is accomplished through special developers and by different developing times which will be discussed later in the chapter. The term 10X or existing light (10X) photography tells us that such a technique has been used.

TAKING THE PICTURE

It is difficult, to develop simultaneously a group of frames in which some are properly exposed and others are underexposed. Therefore, all exposures are calculated as underexposures, usually one-tenth the regular value (the 10X number). Then the entire roll will be uniformly underexposed and later developed as a unit so that every frame will be developed to the same degree. Here then is the author's technique:

Exposure is made on the basis of a standardized, 10-time underexposure. A regular exposure meter, and a medium A.S.A. 40 medium-speed film is employed. However, for 10X photography, the A.S.A. indicator is set at 400. All exposures will be made at 1/25 second.

1. The exposure has been standardized at 1/25 second, with an A.S.A. 40 film to be used at ten times its regular speed, or an A.S.A. of 400. The only variable now remaining will be the adjustment of the iris for different light levels.

91

10X—Existing Light—Argus 35mm wide-angle lens.

2. Take a piece of white adhesive tape and place it on your exposure meter scale so that the indicating needle moves past it.

3. Move the reading dial so that the f/1.5 marking is opposite where the needle would have to be if the f/1.5 opening were indicated. Find and mark the position for f/2, 2.8, 4, 5.6, etc. This makes it a direct-reading scale. Whenever the needle points to f/3.5 we know that under a 10X type of photography, film and shutter speed (having been previously standardized) will require an f/3.5 opening. If the needle points opposite f/4, set the iris at f/4, etc. The meter now is calibrated for direct reading 10X photography.

Computation is now perfectly simple because you merely set your iris at what the needle reads.

4. The meter is used then by merely reading it in the normal way (either by reflection or incident light) and taking the iris reading directly from the position of the needle swing on the meter and setting it on the lens.

INDOORS OR SPORTS-TYPE LIGHTING

Indoor-stage or sports-type lighting is often difficult to judge because of your great distance from the light source. Therefore, the author has devised a technique for such conditions which utilizes an extinction-type (Leudi) meter which is calibrated against your regular photo-electric meter when it is used for 10X photography.

The extinction meter is calibrated in this way: In a normally lighted room, read your meter that has been set for 10X photography and note its iris setting. Then look through the extinction meter, and note the clearest number that can be seen. Take a piece of white adhesive tape and calibrate it so that the clearest visible number through it will have the same reading as the photo-electric meter. In this way, the No. 3 may mean an f/4 at 1/25 with an A.S.A. 40 set at 400; the 4 will indicate an f/2.8 at these same conditions, etc.

92

Normal Theatre Lighting
with 10X Factors

After the extinction meter has been calibrated, you can sit any-where in a theatre or sports arena and use it to read the correct exposure. Since this meter is not as exact as a photo-electric meter (because of the variable light level adjustments possible with your eyes), try a test roll with it before you trust the readings implicitly. In any case, record your results for future standardization or shift the markings into an accurate position.

Focus must be exact because your lens, as we know now, has limited depth of sharpness at its wider openings. The Safe-Set Method is applicable because it is far easier to pre-set your camera to a definite subject size and move back and forth a bit, than to rotate the focusing knob continuously. Just one turn of the focusing knob, as has been pointed out, can bring you from infinity to 3 feet, whereas a pre-set focusing distance will often be off less than 2 or 3 inches.

Existing-light, or 10X, photography, because a 1/25-second speed is routine, requires that you know your subject thoroughly so you can catch your action at its peak of effect without any great movement. When photographing a stage play, it is wise to see it once or twice so that you can foretell the climaxes and be ready for them.

Try, whenever possible, to prevent any direct light from shining into the lens. This can be avoided by moving your camera position so that the subject's head blocks any back light from shining towards the lens. A lens shade is also highly desirable because it reduces possible glare and flare to a minimum.

93

Normal Room Lighting With 10X Factors

DEVELOPING THE PICTURE

10X black-and-white negative development differs from the standard developing generally recommended. The reason is this: If the normal developing times are used, the underexposure will result in a thin, unusable negative. To secure a dense negative, we either must increase the developer's energy, increase the developing time, or use specially compounded developers.

At this point, it would be possible to write a treatise on the various chemical modifications capable of increasing the developing energy of any known developer. It would, however, serve no purpose because the average amateur has neither the accessibility nor the inclination to mix his own special solution. Therefore, only those methods that can be used with your everyday normally available developing solutions will be recommended.

Usable negatives. the same as those used for the illustrations are produced by this proven data:

1. Using the replenisher of any standardized fine-grain developer for approximately the same time as you would with the regular developer. Microdol replenisher can be used with 10X photography for approximately 14 minutes. D-76R and D-17R Replenisher should also be used at 14 minutes. The Microdol Replenisher is preferred because it produces a *finer grain* pattern than any of the others. Employ your solutions economically more than once by taking a quart of fresh Microdol Replenisher, dividing it into two pints, using one pint as the stock solution and replenishing from

94

Normal Store Lighting With 10X Factors

the other pint at the rate of 2 ounces for every roll of 120 film. After the second pint is finished, throw all solutions away.

PRINTING THE PICTURE

Because the ideal 10X negative has many of the same characteristics as the normal one, the printing procedures are standard. Greater or lesser contrasts can be produced by changing the grade of paper, the type of printing developer, or the dilution of the stock solution.

If you follow these procedures, 10X photography will revive and restimulate your interest in black-and-white film because of its unique effect, the richness of its tonal scale, and the naturalness of its results.

Note: Low light levels necessitate speeds slower than 1/25 second when the widest lens opening is f/3.5 or f/2.8. For these low intensities, keep your lens wide open and change the shutter speeds only. The principle is to allow only one variable to be changed for standardization of results.

As our everyday records, such as newspapers, legal papers, and books, accumulate, the need for ample storage space and proper preservation of these important documents increases. With the 35mm Argus cameras, you can economically and conveniently make permanent records of this material. Copying and microfilming are easily done after you have established a simple, standard (Safe-Set) procedure.

When you are copying flat surfaces, you must have the back of your camera parallel to the base of the copying stand. This helps to insure perfect image resolution and sharpness. For best results, the upright column of the copying stand should be wide and rigid to prevent vibration, the copy should be kept perfectly flat, and the film should be fine grained.

The many field sizes for various supplementary (Portra-Lenses) as well as the distance scale settings may be found in the Lens Charts. It is much easier to standardize on four distances and mark your copying stand column so that your camera may be moved from one position to another instantly. The baseboard of the copying stand should be marked to co-ordinate with the column heights. Do this by following the directions below.

1. Mount your camera and raise it to the highest point on your copying stand.

2. Drop a plumb line or a weighted string directly from the center of your supplementary lens that has been placed over your camera lens.

3. Mark this reference point on the baseboard.

4. With this point as center, draw a rectangle 8 by 12 inches, making the 12-inch side parallel with the long horizontal side of your film.

5. Draw small rectangles in the proportion of 1:1½. Use those sizes which you think you will need most often, e.g., 4 x 6 inches, 5 x 7½ inches, etc.

6. Prepare a chart which will carry the co-ordinated field size, supplementary lens, and column height markings. Fix this chart permanently on the baseboard of your copying stand.

7. Use a glass plate to keep your copy flat.

Since most documents are black on white, it is very practical and economical to use fine-grained positive film, in bulk, for photographing them. This film need not be developed to a positive because of

FACTS ABOUT COLOR

Our studies of color can be standardized by differentiating each color in three ways:

Hue. This is the distinguishing name of a color, such as red, yellow, or green.

Value. This means the lightness or darkness of a color as compared with a white to black scale; for example: light green, medium green, dark green.

Chroma. This indicates the brilliance or purity of a color after it is toned down with gray; for example, orange to brown.

Selection of Color for Special Effects

Harmonious colors adjoin one another on the hue circuit (color wheel); light green will harmonize with lemon yellow or deep green.

Contrasting colors are directly opposite each other on the color wheel; for example, lemon yellow contrasts with brilliant purple, or flame red with peacock blue.

Triadic color combinations can be made by starting a single color and then drawing a triangle with two equal sides. The colors that occur at the three points of the triangle can be used together. Lemon yellow, flame red, and peacock blue or brilliant purple, orange and deep green are a few of the possible triadic combinations.

Simultaneous contrasting color combinations enhance one another beyond the usual degree of contrast when the proportions of their sizes and designs are varied. By covering the black square in the center of the wheel, the gray square seems lighter; covering the white square makes the gray seem darker. Illustrations 7A, 7B, 8A and 8B demonstrate this clearly.

Greater contrast, as shown in illustrations 10, and 11, is best produced by selecting colors of strong (brilliant) chroma

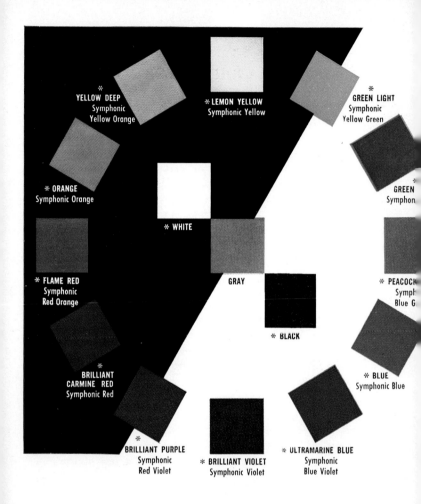

* YELLOW DEEP
Symphonic
Yellow Orange

* LEMON YELLOW
Symphonic Yellow

* GREEN LIGHT
Symphonic
Yellow Green

* ORANGE
Symphonic Orange

GREEN
Symphon

* WHITE

* FLAME RED
Symphonic
Red Orange

GRAY

* PEACOCK
Symph
Blue G

* BLACK

* BLUE
Symphonic Blue

* BRILLIANT
CARMINE RED
Symphonic Red

* BRILLIANT PURPLE
Symphonic
Red Violet

* BRILLIANT VIOLET
Symphonic Violet

* ULTRAMARINE BLUE
Symphonic
Blue Violet

*"Color Wheel courtesy of M. Grumbacher, Inc.,
manufacturer of Phototint and Artists' Colors."*

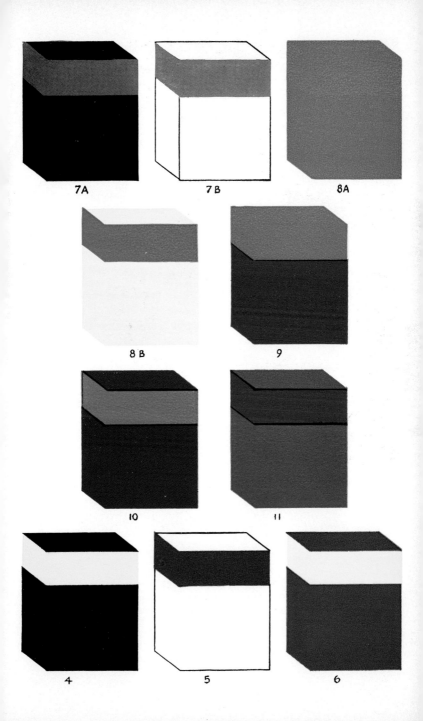

7A　　　　7B　　　　8A

8B　　　　9

10　　　　11

4　　　　5　　　　6

that have marked difference in value. Some of the possibilities are lemon yellow with black, ultramarine blue with white, and light green with brilliant violet.

Similarity of chroma and value causes a competitive disharmony that destroys the pleasant effect (see illustration 9). The chroma of one color should be weakened so that the other color will appear brighter and more dominant by comparison.

Visibility and legibility results when colors are chosen that have the greatest contrast in value. In illustrations 4, 5, and 6, it can be easily seen that a high, almost white, dilution contrasts best with a color of strong chroma (brilliance) which is without dilution (or vice versa).

Application of Color to Photography

The three dimensions of color — hue, value, and chroma — must be applied efficiently when making a picture because color harmonies and contrasts are just as important in securing the final effect as are the technical and composition factors. For instance, a movie of children should be decorated with colors of light value, whereas a drama is usually costumed and decorated with colors of darker value. You will find it helpful to spend a day at a museum of art where you can study the many practical and different applications of the color theory.

the great legibility and contrast of typewritten or printed matter. The developed negative will show white lettering on a black background and is easily read. However, when color originals are to be copied, then a micro-type panchromatic emulsion with an ASA 8 is the film to choose. Light balancing in copying is very important in that your illumination must always be perfectly even in all directions. Unevenness in illumination is distracting and, in addition, distorts the tonal values of either color or black and white continuous tone originals. Use a meter to assure evenness of illumination and to correct any hot spots on your subject matter. A certain amount of glare can be reduced through the use of a polar screen (polarizing filter) on your camera lens. If your printed material is glossy you can polarize your illuminating lights and also use a polarizing filter on the camera.

If your illumination is so even as to smoothly cover your largest field size, then you will not need to change your exposure factors as your field areas differ. The best way to achieve even illumination is by keeping light sources independent of camera movement. If your lights are attached to your camera, then as the camera moves up and down, your light position changes and a new exposure must be calculated for each new camera-to-subject distance. Note that once the information for each basic light placement as well as your camera height to field size distances have been tabulated, re-computations will never be necessary for the same equipment used in the same way. It is a simple matter then to take your camera, mount it on the copying stand, turn on your pre-set lights and start your copying or microfilming.

CHAPTER 22 / **SLIDES AND THEIR PROJECTION**

Many amateurs like to work with slides in color because of the simplicity and ease of slide production, and the absence of darkroom work. If the beginner will follow the illustrations and instructions of Chapter 1, he will produce excellent slides. But, since color limits your after-control of the returned transparency, it is imperative that you do everything correctly from the beginning of the picture taking process. When the color transparency is returned to you, there are still many steps required for its transformation into a color slide of lasting value. You should first edit and then keep only those slides which approach perfection. A bad slide is a bad slide regardless of the fact that it might have been taken in color. However, an excellent

97

slide should receive all the care and attention possible. If your slides are to be used much, it is wise to remove the transparency from the paper binding in which they are returned by the processing laboratory and remount them. You should do your remounting in a dust-free room. It is a good idea to wear cotton gloves to avoid smudging or scratching. To clean glass slides before mounting, follow the procedure outlined below:

1. Mix a small quantity of Oakite, Calgon or other detergent in a basin of warm water.

2. Place your glass slides into the water and move them around so that the glass is evenly wet on all sides.

3. Allow fresh water to flow into the basin for at least ten minutes. This will wash out the detergent and leave only pure water.

4. Dry each glass with a lintless cloth, and set it into a grooved rack or stand it against a dust free book.

5. A static eliminating brush (static-master) may be used to remove any dust particles that remain. This brush will at the same time set up a static charge which will repel any more dust.

6. Use this brush to remove all particles of dust from your film, masks, etc.

7. You may use masks with aluminum edge binders or bind your own masks with the illustrated Binding Button.

Purchase a slide box that is sturdy enough to protect the glass slides when they are in transit. You may print black-and-white transparencies or you can order enlargements so that your composition and subject rendition may be improved. Black-and-white transparencies may also be toned and hand colored, a process which will do much to improve the negative's possibilities.

With color, simple after-treatment is limited to cropping by the use of masking tape. Some color correction is possible in a limited manner through the use of Add-a-color. (See Chapter 25).

Once your glass slide has been bound, it may be used in a variety of ways:

1. *Hand viewer*. Illumination may be built in or ceiling light and natural light may be utilized by reflection. A recent innovation, the small telescope viewer, produces an effect that has a great deal of novelty.

2. *Electric pre-viewer*. For sorting, correcting, and editing your collection.

3. *Table viewer*. A convenient table-size projection viewer enables you to see the enlarged slide under regular room light. No

elaborate set-up is required. The illustrations demonstrate the simplicity of this method.

4. *Projection.* Argus, Incorporated supplies a complete line of projectors for satisfying many needs. Many models also have a conversion unit for using both film strips and glass slides.

5. *Color enlargements.* The Eastman Kodak Company's Kodacolor Prints and Ansco Printons may be made from your 35mm Kodachromes or Ansco Color Transparencies. These enlargements have an opaque white backing and may be viewed by reflected light only. Enlargements up to 8x10 inches and 11x14 inches may be made. However, it is important to emphasize that the color of the enlargements will not exactly duplicate that of the original transparencies. But since there is no other process available at the moment, the manufacturers and processors take as much care as possible to maintain a high color standard.

6. Special table transparency frames (Lumax) are available which reflect the room light from the ceiling onto the transparency by means of an aluminum surface which is placed behind the transparency at a light-catching angle. The picture size that you see is limited to the size of the transparency.

SLIDE PRESENTATION

The presentation of your slides for viewing is very important in maintaining the interest of your audience. You must become a showman and make your pictures tell the story. Write a script which will co-ordinate your slides so that they have a unified effect. If the script is long and difficult to remember, then tape record it for your convenience. Once you have edited your slides and script, you can expect to receive many invitations to put on your show. When this happens you will know that, as a photographer, you have "arrived."

Argus Automatic Slide Changer.

Argus Expandable Slide Magazine Carrying Case. One thousand eighty individual color slides can be conveniently collected in one case.

Argus Stereo Slide Carrier. Fits the Argus Projector and permits easy projection of a single frame of any type stereo slide.

Thirty-five millimeter stereo (three-dimensional photography) has been a continuing source of interest to photographers and has provided a field for a good deal of experimentation. The owner of a 35mm camera is fortunate in that his standardized taking and viewing equipment (Realist or Verascope viewers; Leica or Rolleiflex shift bar) is suitable for stereo photography.

Why do you see depth with stereo? This is the question most frequently asked about stereo photography by the beginner.

This is the explanation: You have two eyes. The separation of the eyes generally is 65mm (2⅝ inches). Because of this, each eye does not see exactly the same scene as the other. Since the eyes are separated by 65mm, the view of each eye is offset by this separating distance. This difference in viewpoint is known as parallax. If you have ever fired a gun, you realize that you must correct for the difference between your line of sight and that of the bore of the gun muzzle. If you do not compensate for this difference, you will always miss your target if your eye cannot be made to see the same view of your target as the gun bore. It is precisely this difference in viewpoint (parallax), however, that makes depth perception possible with stereo. Because when each eye records and transmits a slightly different viewpoint to your brain, a fusion of the two images occurs. The result of the fusion and co-ordination of the different viewpoints into a continuous smooth picture is depth perception.

With one eye, you can see only a flat picture because there is only one viewpoint. If you take two pictures which are exactly alike without moving the camera at all and view them in the stereo viewer, the scene will still be flat. You must "triangulate"—that is, you must see each scene from two different points of view in order to be able to duplicate the depth effect of your eyes. Depth perception is possible only when the two images are taken from two different viewpoints. The difference in viewpoint may be minute, as little as one tenth of an inch apart for close distances. On the other hand for long distances, the separation for the two different exposures may be yards or even miles. There are formulas for calculating the taking separation distances. You will be shown how to calculate the distance between paired exposures so that you may be able to produce excellent depth perception for any distances.

You can take stereos with your 35mm camera by any of the three following practical methods:

Stereo-tach Illuminated Viewer

1. *1/50 formula (projection)*—1/25 (viewing) shift bar for still subjects only. The theoretically ideal studio effect has been calculated to result from an inter-lens separation which is 1/50 of the camera-to-subject distance. As you come closer to the subject (24 inches or less) this separation must become greater in order to secure a better modeling of the subject.

When the camera is used according to the shift bar formula, two frame arrangements are possible:

(a.) *Horizontal format*—taken by shifting the camera with the long side of the film horizontal. The finished transparencies may be viewed in the Busch Variscope viewer. The dimensions of the Busch viewer mask opening are 24x30mm. The amount of film area lost is only three millimeters from each side. Masks, which permit you to mount your transparency easily, have indicating marks to insure perfect interocular separation for the finished slide.

(b.) *Vertical format*—will yield transparencies which are suitable for the Realist viewer (22x24mm). This format poses two problems. First the film must be cut in a horizontal plane and the transparencies mounted in precise alignment so that there is no "twisting." Second, it is necessary to mask your viewfinder to cover the field of view. You must standardize your viewfinding methods so that all your transparencies can be mounted alike.

The horizontal format is the simplest. Standard masks for mount-

Stereo-tach on the C-3

ing transparencies taken in this manner are always available. You make your stereo pairs by using your camera on a sliding shift bar for two separate exposures. With this bar, the 1/50 formula is used in the following way. You measure your subject-to-lens distance. If the subject is 40 inches from your lens, the interocular distance between exposures will be 4/5 of an inch. You focus and compose your picture and then ready the camera for the exposure. Then, shift the camera to the left for half the needed distance (2/5 of an inch for this example), take your picture, rewind it and again cock your shutter, etc. Then shift your camera to the right for the full distance. In this way, your viewed image will be exact and the distance shifted will be correct. It is important to understand that only by shifting equally on both sides of your center point will your viewed image and your final stereo be alike.

If the subject-to-lens distance is 20 inches, then the separating point will be 2/5 inch, etc. In using a shift bar you must remember the sequence of the exposures that are being made. You must also remember to change your supplementary lenses as you come closer in order to keep your subject in focus. In addition, you must correct for viewfinder parallax at close distances. If you intend to take many close-ups, then you may construct a permanent stand with markings for the exact focusing distance. Should the depth produced by the 1/50 shift prove inadequate for your needs, then you may try a formula based on 1/25 or 1/12.5 distance. This will increase the separation of your two exposures. The increased separation will pro-

103

duce a greater amount of triangulation, and this in turn will produce the greater stereo effect.

2. *Two-camera method*. A moving subject can be taken only through the simultaneous use of two cameras. Again there is a choice of horizontal or vertical formats. If you use the horizontal format, your center-to-center lens separation is about four inches. If a subject is taken at a short distance, the increased lens separation from the normal 2⅝ inch distance will make viewing more difficult.

As the vertical arrangement permits an approximately 2⅝ inch center-to-center lens separation, I recommend the following arrangement. Two vertical cameras are arranged so that both their base plates are together. Since two cameras are difficult to focus, manipulate, etc., it is best to set your shutter and iris combinations for the use of your hyper-focal distance or according to the depth of field charts. In this manner, you will be assured of a sharp, co-ordinated picture by once again using the Safe-Set Method.

3. *The Stereo-Tach Reflector Method*. This unique device is the most practical method for the amateur. The Stereo-tach system consists of four front-surfaced mirrors which are so arranged that two separate images are formed from two differing viewpoints separated by the normal inter-eye distance of 65mm. Both of these different images are formed on only one full film frame (24x36mm). Each image size, half of the pair, is approximately 18x24mm. The use of the Stereo-tach is economical because both images are formed together on only one full frame. In order to view this Stereo-tach transparency, the special Stereo-tach viewer (which is a reverse of the taking mirror arrangement) must be used. However, each frame may be cut apart and the halves remounted in the standard Realist type mask. The recommended taking distance with the Stereo-tach is ten feet. At shorter distances, the angles of the subject reflection from the mirrors form images which are difficult to view. Since both pictures are taken at the same time, the Stereo-tach method is suitable for taking moving subjects.

If the camera lens mount rotates in focusing, the Stereo-tach will rotate with the lens and will produce a poor stereo. You can minimize lens rotation in focusing by the use of your hyper-focal distance or depth of field scales. Set the distance, etc., according to the Safe-Set Method and be sure the Stereo-tach is perfectly level on the camera. You may use the Stereo-tach viewfinder, or you may mask your camera's viewfinder with two pieces of scotch tape so that each will

104

cover ¼ the horizontal measurement of your viewfinder; the middle half in the center will be clear and is the only portion used.

A limitation of viewing stereo with a hand viewer is that only one person at a time can view your transparency. The best method of mass viewing is by the use of polarizing materials and spectacles. These polarizers are placed over each separate view in the optical system, so that one eye will see its polarized view at one angle and the other eye will see the other polarized view at the opposite angle. Co-ordinating polarizing spectacles are worn over both eyes which permit each eye to see only its own respective view without any interference from the other eye's image. When each eye sees its specific view only, the brain fuses the two images so that you see the subject in depth.

There are two methods for stereo projection:

1. Using the Stereo Realist or TDC Stereo Projector. These are two-lens projectors. Each lens projects only one polarized image. Either projector will take the full 35mm 24x36mm size, and the resulting projection size may be as large as 5 feet by 5 feet.

2. Taylor Stereo Table Viewer. This is a small projector, conveniently designed for table use with regular room light.

3. Since you view the Stereo-tach transparency by reversing the taking device (the Stereo-tach viewer), projection is likewise possible by projecting our scene back through the Stereo-tach taking device. *But, this image synthesis (re-forming) is possible only if the projector lens has the same focal length as the camera lens.* If the stereo was taken with a 2-inch lens, it must be projected with a 2-inch lens, so that the proportion of taking and viewing perspective are carefully maintained. If a 44mm camera lens was used, then a 44mm projecting lens must be used. If you try to use a projection lens of longer or shorter focal length than was used on the camera, your two screen images (from each stereo half) will be so far apart that your eyes cannot fuse the separated images to re-form the picture in depth.

Only the polarization method of projection will permit color to retain its true identity. Many people claim that color is the only thing that makes our everyday surroundings interesting. By using your 35mm camera for stereo, you are able to recapture this interest in a life-like form. No matter what taking method is used, stereo always is worthy of a trial. Its real-life quality and dramatic depth will enable you to realize another potentiality for pleasure with your camera.

You can interpret your subject by either existing, bounce and direct light. Each light will produce a different effect:

Existing Light. The subject is photographed under the actual light of his environment. This light may be so dim that special developers and developing methods must be used to overcome the inertia threshold of your film in order to produce a picture. With existing light, your subject is natural because there are no distracting, unusual looking gadgets on the camera. The camera is portable because there is no added weight, and sequence pictures may be taken easily. Since the subject is at ease, the pictures are more natural and spontaneous.

Bounce Light. A photoflood is generally placed on a tall stand and the light reflected against the ceiling. In effect, the ceiling acts as a huge diffusing reflector. The resulting light is in many instances similar to your regular room light. Bounce light has a tendency to soften contrasts and I would, therefore, suggest a 20 percent increase in development time. In addition, take care that your body does not stop the bounce light rays from reaching your subject. This is especially important if you are at the closer taking distances. You can overcome this shielding effect by taking your pictures from a kneeling or squatting position. Use the bounce-strobe or bounce-flash in a similar manner. Since a light reading cannot be made with a photo-electric meter of your ceiling reflected strobe or flash exposures, I have found that if you divide your normal exposure (calculated for a direct light-to-subject distance) by 4, your exposure will be correct for a room with an average white ceiling. As an example, if your normal direct flash or strobe would require an f/11 opening, with a bounce light technique the exposure opening to use will be f/5.6.

Direct Light. This has been the regular method for picture taking. The appearance of your subject gives a contrived impression in that the shadows seem to be "tailor made." However, when you must be certain of an exposure or a picture, the direct method of lighting will produce a greater uniformity of results.

The charts at the back of the book suggests the film speeds, regular and special developers, and developing times, for any method that you may choose.

Film with higher A.S.A. speeds necessitate meter settings that are higher for added speed with the special existing light techniques.   →

106

FACTS FOR INDOOR ARTIFICIAL LIGHT TECHNIQUE - FILM ASA 40

Type of Light		Use Film at ASA Speed	Developer at 68° F.	Condenser	Diffuser	Suggestions
Existing	High Meter can be read	ASA 40	D-76 DK-20	9-16 minutes	11-13 minutes	Shield direct light behind a sign, post or person
	Low-Dim Low Meter reading (if at all)	ASA 400	D-76 ÷ borax Promicrol	7 1/2-11 12±	9 14±	Experiment with subjects 4 to 10 feet from a 40, 100, 200 watt bulb. Lens wide open at slow speeds up to 1/25 seconds
			Additional speed can be gotten by developing to 15 minutes or more			
Bounce light reflected from ceiling or wall	Flood	ASA 40 When meter can be read	D-76 DK-20	15 16	17 18	Low diffused light subject contrast requires No.3 or No.4 paper
	Flash	Guide No.ASA 10	D-76 DK-20	15 16	17 18	As above
	Strobe	Guide No.ASA 10	D-76 DK-20	18 19	20 21	Print normal
Directed	Flood	ASA 40	D-76 DK-20	11 12	13 14	Use I-G-A-S formula to balance your light volumes
	Flash	Guide No.ASA 40	D-76 DK-20	10 11	12 13	Use correct reflectors, avoid "hot spots"
	Strobe	150-watt-second Flash Guide No.90	D-76 DK-20	11 12	13 14	Print on No.3 or No.4 paper
	Strobe	150-watt-second Flash Guide No.150	D-76 DK-20 DK-60a	18 19 7	19 20 8	Choose correct paper grade carefully

Photomicrography, as you know, is the photographic recording of minute subjects that can only be seen with a microscope. The miniature camera enables you to take pictures of microscopic material with ease. Before you load your camera with film, it is best to calibrate your camera with the back removed. The ideal relationship of camera to microscope is determined by the following method:

1. Remove the back of the camera.
2. Focus the regular lens at infinity with iris wide open.
3. Focus the microscope visually.
4. Insert the microscope adapter ring (author's design) into a filter holder and secure it with a regular retaining ring.
5. Place the filter holder combination over the camera lens, so that the film is perfectly parallel with the microscope slide. Place the camera and the microscope filter assembly over the microscope lens (which should never be removed from the microscope barrel).
6. Place a piece of ground glass or thin paraffin paper on top of the camera's mask opening. See if the image is sharp.
7. Magnifying lens may be used.
8. If the image is blurred, move your microscope toward you or refocus the microscope until the image is in sharp focus. Note the amount of extension. If necessary start your original focus with the drawtube slightly extended and note the amount of drawtube contraction necessary to bring the image to sharp focus. Write down this information so that you will have the necessary extension or contractor factor available when you need it.

Once this information has been tabulated, then load your camera with any of the following film materials and use the suggested light sources.

The photographic image produced by this method does not fill the entire negative area, but a five-times enlargement of your negative film image will re-constitute the proportions of the final print to the same eye viewing ratio which is necessary for 10-inch viewing. Since your photo-micrograph was taken with a 1¾-inch lens (Signet 35) or the regular 2-inch lens, a five-times magnification (5 times 2 inches) duplicates your normal 10-inch viewing distance.

Camera owners who have electronic flash are encouraged to experiment with this light form. Electronic flash produces an intense light without any heat, which makes it a desirable source of light.

Standardize all your picture-taking factors. Measure the distance of your light source from the microscope mirror and record it. Although it may seem to you that the position of the light is changed only a few inches, remember that, according to the inverse-square light rule, these few inches forward or back may increase or decrease your light volume as much as four times. Since color film has a limited latitude of ½ to 1 stop, this four-times factor can cause serious under- or over-exposure. By measuring and recording your light distance, you can be sure of a uniformity of exposure.

Argus used for photomicrography

Kodachrome or Ansco color films are generally sent to a laboratory for processing, and since a month may elapse before your transparencies are returned, it is best to record your complete picture-taking information. Unless you have made notes of your procedure, you will have no basis for future work.

FILM AND EXPOSURE CHART

LIGHT SOURCE: *T-10, tungsten ribbon filament, 18-amp. 6-volt lamp; carbon arc, electronic flash*

Film	Kodak Filter	Subject	My Exposure Information:
B & W Positive Blue Sensitive	None	Black, white, gray	
B & W Finopan Superior 1	Wratten B	Panchromatic; any colored stain	
Color Indoor Ansco Color	None	All true colors	
Color Koda-chrome, Type A	Light Balancing No. 82A	All natural colors	

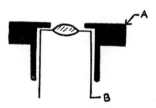

MICROSCOPE ADAPTER (A) IS PLACED INTO A STANDARD FILTER HOLDER THAT FITS INTO THE REGULAR CAMERA LENS. THE WHOLE ASSEMBLY IS SEATED ONTO THE MICROSCOPE BARREL (B)

EXISTING LIGHT EXPOSURE TABLE

A.S.A. 400 Setting for A.S.A 40 film, using X-33 Replenisher full strength for 10 minutes at 68°F.		
Light Strength	*Subject Distance*	*Suggested Settings*
25 watt	4'	f/3.5 - 1/2 sec.
40 watt	4'	f/3.5 - 1/5
140 watt	4'	f/4 - 1/10 or f/2.8 - 1/25
500 watt, PS 25 directed at a white ceiling	Anywheres in a 10' room	f/3.5 - 1/50 or f/4.5 - 1/25
2RFL2 directed at a white ceiling	Anywheres in a 10' room	f/4.5 - 1/50 or f/6.3 - 1/25

The Argus PreViewer. A magnified, wide field image is produced which can be viewed by two or more persons.

Accura Universal and close-up view-finder is parallax corrected to 10".

Koiled Kord Flash attachment for an off-the-camera better modeling effect.

The Polyco Ground Glass should be used to check the precise focusing distance of any portrait lens or extension tube. (Courtesy *Photographic Importing and Distributing Corp.*)

It is very easy to learn proper landscape color balance by studying Mother Nature. You will always find that the backgrounds of your color slides are blue and the foregrounds lean towards the reds.

Backgrounds should be blue to appear normal. Blue colors are known as receding colors.

Foregrounds may be red. The warm colors are known as advancing colors. While a sunset is further than your mountains, the warm color leaves you with the impression of closeness compared to the nearer (in miles) mountain.

Contrast can be chosen by selecting complementary colors on your color wheel (hue circuit).

Warm tones are colors of red or orange. To further warm a color, add more of a warm color.

Cold tones are colors of blue or green. To further cool a color, add cooler colors.

Direct opposites on a color wheel generally harmonize.

1. Equal subject color areas produce competing areas of attraction.

2. Unequal subject color areas are desirable to provide a center of interest.

3. Outdoors if your sky value is too high compared to your subject value, then the higher contrast will always draw the center of interest. Wait for a hazy sky to lower the contrast and so shift the attention to your subject.

This is the era of color, but the full potentialities are yet to be fully realized. The subject is so vast that this text can serve only as an introduction to further study. Practical considerations have been given priority in order to give sufficient information about basic color theory so that you can use this material in everyday picture-taking.

Before any house is built, a foundation must be formed. Similarly the foundation for color must start by breaking down the complex mixtures to the elementary colors in their simplest form. The building-block colors are known as primary colors. There are only *three* primary colors, but these may be of two *types:*

113

MEN:	CLOTHING	BACKGROUND
	Gray	Dull blue, buff or tan
	Black	Any lighter color for neutral effect
	Blue-gray	Neutral tan
	Brown	Blue-gray, buff, or olive green
	Tan	Blue-gray, buff, or olive green
	Khaki	Dark green
	Blue	Buff or gray
	Yellow	Violet or blue-gray
WOMEN:	Lavender	Gray-green
	Blue	Yellow, darker blue, blue green or red
	Green	Darker green, gray, lavender, maroon, red or blue
	Yellow	Gray-blue, violet, blue
	Pink	Dull blue
	Red	Green, blue, or blue-green
	White	Light contrasty shades for delicacy; dark contrasty shades for mood; never yellow
	Maroon	Gray-blue, blue-green
	Gray	Maroon or brighter blue

CHILDREN:	CLOTHING	BACKGROUND
	Pink	Blue or green
	Blue	Coral, pale pink or white
	Yellow	Green, blue-green
	White	Pale blue or other pastels

	HIGH CONTRAST	LOW CONTRAST	SIMULTANEOUS CONTRAST
HUE (Color)	Opposite ends of a color wheel	Adjoining	Appears lighter against dark backgrounds Appears darker against light backgrounds Complementary hues appear more brilliant next to each other
VALUE (bright)	Differing	Similar	Similar, cause competition; differing, for best viewing
CHROMA (gray)	Strong	Weak	Stronger, appears more brilliant next to a weaker chroma

114

1. If you are *adding* primary colors to get a white light, Primary-Blue + Green + Red = White. When any two primary colors are combined, they form a new complementary color to the third, remaining primary. Complementary: Magenta (Green + Red), Cyan (Blue + Green), Yellow, (Green + Blue).

2. If you are *subtracting* primary colors from white light to leave a black (absence of light): Magenta + Cyan + Yellow = Black. The complementaries are: Green (Cyan + Yellow); Orange (Yellow + Magenta); Purple Cyan and Magenta).

Colors are identified by:

1. Hue-color: the distinguishing of colors as you see them—red, green, blue, yellow, etc. Using the combined word hue-color will simplify for the beginner what is meant by hue.

2. Value—bright: dark, middle or light, refers to the relative brightness of a color as it is mixed with white (tint) or black (shade).

3. Chroma—gray: strong, moderate, or weak, refers to the relative brilliance of a mixture of a hue-color which is subdued when differing proportions of gray are added.

The combining of the first two words has been purposeful in order to have the beginner associate the two important words and so be able to better understand and describe the balancing of the three different color factors.

Color Harmony

The color harmony that is detailed here is objective although the pleasing grouping of colors is, in many cases, a purely subjective reaction. Because of this subjective reaction, many great painters died penniless when the world lagged far behind in appreciating their bold new color effects or color harmony.

In using this chart, you will produce classically correct color harmony. While these harmonies are conservative, they will serve as a starting point for more daring attempts.

The most frequent color slide subjects are people. While the color harmony mentioned is for men, women and children, slight alterations may make them applicable for inanimate subjects. These harmonies are not rigid and inflexible. You still must exercise judgment for the hue, chroma, and value, because of the age, appearance, proportions and dress of your subject.

Brightness, brilliance, and gayety are the trade marks of childhood and youth. For this reason, children's clothing ought to be very light with pastels predominating. Little boys should be clothed in blue, little girls in pink, with very few attention-attracting designs or patterns on the clothes to mar the effect of pure simplicity.

A contrasting accenting effect may be secured for little girls by permitting them to wear a hair ribbon which must blend with the color scheme. In keeping with the spirit of the high-key effect, the tint of the background ought to be light while the hue-color must be of the proper color contrast.

It is very important that your subject be in front and well separated from your background by a generous distance. If the subject is light in tone and situated too close to the background, the light tone of the clothing or surface will reflect the different hue-color of the background and so degrade its own color. To prove this take a piece of white satin material and place it next to bright, different hue-colors. You will be surprised to see that the satin reflects a different hue-color whenever it is placed next to a different hue. If the close position of a subject and background is unavoidable, then a polarizing filter must be used to limit the unwanted reflection of the background from your subject and so keep the hue-color purity of the subject and the background distinct from each other.

COLOR CORRECTION

Since the exposure for color must be correct to within very narrow latitudes, it is natural to find exposure errors cropping up from time to time. If you know beforehand that an exposure error has been made with Ansco Color, then this over- or under-exposure information may be sent with your film so the processer can adjust the first developing time to compensate for the error. With Kodachrome, known exposure error information may be relayed to Eastman, for their consideration. However, once your transparency has been developed and returned and you then discover your error, the only means for correction that the amateur may use is through

116

Addacolor. Addacolor is a method whereby you bind differently colored sheets of colored gelatin directly to your transparency. The choice of Addacolor will correct and control your transparency color so as to make up for certain minor deficiencies of exposure or incorrect light source $(K°)$.

Transparency	Addacolor
Too Blue	Yellow
Too Green	Red
Too Yellow	Blue
Too Red	Green

Another advantage of Addacolor is that it permits an over-correction towards a warmer or cooler color for individual interpretation. The simplicity of the procedure makes it ideal. This method is a definite aid which will save many priceless transparencies that would otherwise be discarded.

The great advantages of the miniature camera are its portability, its great depth of field, the sharp definition and the speed of its lens. To best realize the benefits of this maneuverability for portraiture, the camera should be hand held at 1/25 second. If there is very little light available, as for example with a single house lamp, or if the use of color is contemplated, a tripod should be used.

In portraiture, you can take advantage of the miniature camera's portability. Remember that a good portrait must reflect some of the inner qualities of the subject, whether it be a child, an adult or even a pet. Capturing the personality of your subject on film must begin in a pervading atmosphere of relaxation. To set the stage for a pleasant session, your equipment must be all set for use before the subject arrives. You can understand how irritating it can be for your subject to wait for: film to be loaded; camera accessories corrected; picture taking area cleared; suitable chair or bench found; blinding lights turned on and off at intervals; numerous experimental light placements from different positions. A helpful suggestion for the amateur as well as for the professional is to have the room completely illuminated before the subject enters. In an illuminated room, your subject will rapidly accustom himself to the high light level. If the room is dark, your subject's eye muscles are relaxed. As soon as you turn on the high-powered floods, the sudden blinding rays of light will so contract the eye muscles that they may go into spasm. It may take a few minutes for this to pass, and in the meantime the subject is hardly in any mood for picture taking.

To avoid confusing camera control changes during a sitting, you should again use the Safe-Set Method as follows:

1. Pre-set your shutter at 1/5 second for adults, 1/25 second for children or pets. (Camera should be on a tripod.)

2. Set your iris at f/8 for adults, and f/4.5 for children.

3. Choose the correct camera-to-subject distance from the chart in Chapter 1 and set your distance scale. Ideal perspective is at 5 feet.

4. Leave the settings alone.

5. Many geometric patterns for light placement have been suggested but they are often involved. To simplify the multi-light patterns, I use a method which I call the Y-Formation. You simply visualize a letter Y which is made by the light at the camera and the subject forming the base, and two additional lights placed at a 45-

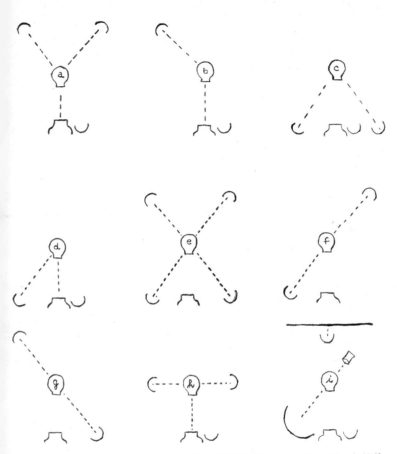

Light arrangement chart a. Y-lighting b. Half Y-lighting c. Arrowhead d. Half-arrowhead e. X-lighting f. See-saw left g. See-saw right h. T-lighting i. Classic lighting

119

degree angle in back of and away from your subject. (See illustration.) This lighting arrangement insures a fully exposed picture combined with excellent subject-from-background separation, as well as interesting highlights. Have all your lights ready and the extension connections in place. The light shade (lens hood) is a necessity for your lens because of back lighting. Take your Y base (illuminating) light and move it so your subject will have an exposure meter reading for this light to indicate the f/8 at 1/5 second setting. If, for example, the light distance measures 6 feet from your subject, then keep this 6 foot distance constant no matter how you may later vary the direction of the main light. For children the light may be adjusted for an f/4.5, 1/25 second exposure. The Y-Formation is especially suitable for children, since there is always an excellent pattern and sufficient light no matter which way they turn.

6.   When the light placement preliminaries are over, sit your subject (plainly dressed, otherwise too much attention may be drawn to the clothes) on a backless stool. This stool is preferable to a chair because it prevents your subject from slumping.

7.   The subject should be at least 6 feet from the background. The problem of subject placement in an apartment where there is not sufficient room for lights, background spacing and freedom of movement can be met by locating the stool in the archway between two rooms. This provides sufficient space from the back wall so that the background light balancing ratio could be changed to any shade. The I-G-A-S formula has demonstrated this effect. In case the background will not materially aid the picture effect, no light should be used. It will then photograph completely black.

8.   Now finish the height and angle placement of the lights. Take the first base light (at the beginning of the Y, in a direct line with your subject) and raise it to the eye level of your subject.

9.   With the remaining two lights (assuming they are the same strength and in the same type of reflector) form the arms of the Y away from the center of your subject. Raise each light about a foot and a half above the head of your subject and point them towards the ears.

10.   In miniature camera portraiture, you seek a natural expression. Photographic speed is not an absolute necessity if you can catch a child or an adult at the height of a motion or expression. It may be difficult to photograph the child while he is in the process of throwing a ball, skipping rope, etc., but if you wait until the hand is fully drawn back before the ball is released, or until the child jumps up and mo-

120

Contemplation at meal time.

Making a Test Light

121

mentarily halts in the air while the rope is passing underneath, you can stop this motion at a relatively slow speed and still get an excellent, blurless picture. A child or pet may be confined to a play pen, high chair, crib, or bench in order to limit the area of activity. Anyone who has tried to photograph an active child on a wide lawn, knows how difficult it is to make the child stay put.

From the basic Y-Formation, countless variations are possible for different effects. If the lights at the ends of the arms of the Y are swung in an arc, then the lights are in a T-Formation. At this angle, your lights will reveal subject texture to best advantage. If the arc is continued forward so that the placement of the three lights in relationship to your subject has the appearance of an arrowhead, you then have a classic 45-degree light placement. For any angle variation from the floor, eye-level or higher position, consult Chapter 16 for a preview of the effect. If you actually wish to visualize what effect any light will have, I suggest the use of a test light (first described by John Alton) for your subject. A test light can be made from a night light that is sold in all hardware stores. In addition, a male prong (illustration) electrical adapter must be used. Take the bulb out of the regular photographic clamp handle, and insert the male adapter with the night lamp in it. Turn off or lower your room lights so that you may see the test effect, because the night lamp is only $7\frac{1}{2}$ watts. By moving the light around your subject, the best position will soon be found. When you have ascertained the ideal direction, place your regular lights and ask your subject to close his eyes so that you can turn on the lights. After a moment, he may open his eyes without the usual discomfort when bright lights are turned full on suddenly.

Flashlight for portraiture is ideal because of the rapidity of the flash coupled with the absence of heat, but the expense involved for each lamp is an important factor. Strobe (electronic flash), on the other hand, is fairly inexpensive to operate, which makes it a good choice for portraiture. The 1/5000 exposure speed certainly is better than the slower speeds used with photofloods, and there is no heat to cause discomfiture. But strobe can be quite tricky to use. A series of tests should be made with your equipment, your filters, and your developing techniques in order to evaluate the correct strobe number. It is helpful to wait double the recharging time that the manufacturer recommends because many of the strobe units I have tested did not deliver their full amount of light even though the indicator light was glowing. For use with color, most strobe units have too low guide numbers, and their color balance is not often reliable. Because of this,

122

you should be cautious in using strobe unless it is of the studio type (Kodatron).

To tie together the information of the different light types with portraiture, it may be of interest to take pictures of grandparents with either direct light, bounce light or existing light (Chapter 23). The older people will definitely not care for the sharper pictures produced by the direct photofloods because their wrinkles will be in sharp outline. With bounce light they will be much softer and more acceptable. Incidentally, bounce light is also recommended for subjects who wear eyeglasses because of the absence of light reflection from the lenses.

For portraiture of small children, a high chair or a blanket covered table with the child carefully held by the mother is ideal. Secure your subject's active co-operation. Adults may smoke a pipe or cigarette, or hold a pencil or book; in other words, do something which will prevent them from becoming conscious of their hands. If their hands are occupied, then that problem will not be so important and in addition the posture of the subject will be more natural. For a child, a ball, a doll, or even a piece of adhesive around a finger will attract him sufficiently to produce interesting characteristic expressions.

Remember that the published pictures that you see are usually chosen from many that have been taken at one sitting. Be encouraged by the fact that the professional photographer may take as many as two or three dozen pictures in the hope of producing one that is typical of the subject. With this in mind, be relaxed, converse with your subject until you learn to anticipate a typical expression. Then, take your picture.

The Safe-Set Method, used with the Y-Formation or its variations, minimizes your attention to the mechanical side of portraiture and lets you concentrate on the far more important aspect—the psychological.

CHAPTER 28 / **MEDICAL AND SCIENTIFIC PHOTOGRAPHY**

S—1/25 ASA 40 Pan, Kodachrome Type A or Ansco Color Tungsten Type.

A—f/openings according to subject—from lights on camera distance.

F—Use the chart in Chapter 1 for head and shoulders, three-

INDOOR FILM - ALL AT 1/25th SECOND

KODACHROME—TYPE F   INDOOR ANSCOCHROME

HORIZONTAL FORMAT Subject Size	Area in Inches	Portra Lens	Camera Distance Setting	Subject to Camera Distance	4RFL2	No. 5 No. 25
Full Body	82"x126"	—	14'	14'	3.5	8
Head and Shoulders	30"x45"	—	5'6"	5'6"	2RFL2 3.5	16
Head	20"x30"	—	3'6"	3'6"	2RFL2 4.5	16
Hand and wrist	6 1/2"x9 1/2"	+2	4'	14"	2RFL2 9	16 4H
Palm	3" x 5"	+5	4'	5-3/4"	2RFL2 11	16 9H
Eye Area	1 1/2"x2-5/8"	+10	4'	3-5/8"	2RFL2 f/16	16 11H

H—Handkerchief — Thin, white, linen — Tests must be made as materials differ widely.

Electronic flash column should be filled after testing your own unit.

Reflector efficiency may change the f/number for your outfit. Change the chart's numbers whenever necessary to suit your equipment.

OUTDOOR FILM - ALL AT 1/25
KODACHROME ANSCO COLOR

Black and White ASA 40

HORIZONTAL FORMAT Subject Size	4RFL2	SM-SF	No.5-No.25	Electronic Flash	5B 25B Electronic	5B 25B Electronic
Full Body	9	5.6	11		4	4
Head and Shoulders	2RFL2 9	12.7	16 1 1/2 H		11	11
Head	2RFL2 16 1H	16 3H	16 3H		15	15
Hand and Wrist	2RFL2 16 3H	::	::		16	16 +4H
Palm	2RFL2 16 4H	::	::		16 +6H	16 +6H
Eye Area	2RFL2 16 6H	::	::		16 8H	16 8H

If film has A.S.A. rating of 80 then set iris one stop narrower.
If film has A.S.A. rating of 25 then set iris approximately one stop wider,

quarters, or full view. For close-ups, the tables for using the Portra or Portrait Lenses with floods, flash, etc. should be used.

For any scientific method of study, a reference point must be used to estimate size or distances. To do this conveniently for your subject size, it is best to take your pictures at known ratios of size reduction. The ratios are generally in the decimal system to make any multiplication or division simple. So, to co-ordinate your information fully:

1. Place a one-inch reference name plate in the plane of your sharpest desirable focus point.

2. Safe-Set your camera and lights for this pre-set distance.

3. Do not touch any control from these settings but move the camera and light set-up back and forth until the sharpest focus is achieved. When the desired composition is seen, release the shutter.

4. Prepare a white cardboard screen ruled with one-inch squares. Project your slide onto this ruled screen so that your one-inch reference name plate enlarges to the size of the cardboard's one inch square. When this occurs, you have a 1:1 relationship. If you project your slide so that your one-inch name plate covers two inches, then your image size is enlarged twice. In all cases, you establish a decimal ratio of reference co-ordination which may be useful in estimating any subject size factor.

If you do not wish to project your image, then you can use calipers to measure your name plate and once your reduction ratio has been established, it is a simple matter to measure (read) any object on your film and quickly calculate its normal size.

The ASA 50 film available in the miniature size will produce a great tonal relationship which approximates the brightness intensity as seen by the eye with the use of an X-1 filter.

Kodachrome Type A, or Ansco Color Tungsten Type are the films preferred for medical and scientific photography in that a diagnosis is generally possible with only the color slide for reference.

The shutter speed should be 1/25 so that most subject movement is stopped. When floodlamps are used, it is wise to turn them on before your subject comes to the photographic field. Test this on yourself and you will find that your eyes can readily attune themselves to a brightly lit scene, while turning your bright lights off and on at rather rapid intervals will rapidly tire them. Should a patient object to any lights, a pair of dark glasses should be available or a handkerchief or towel bound around the head. Our experience has been that if the lights are continually on, no inconvenience will result.

The medical and scientific close-up generally requires an over-all

126

sharp image. This sharpness is produced by narrowing (stopping down) your iris. With color, a light intensity for f/5.6 at 1/25 provides adequate depth of field.

The one-inch name plate may be black and white to offer a fine contrasting focusing target. It may be procured at a professional sign maker. You may use a measured portion of your X-ray marker, or have a jeweler engrave your name on black bakelite or some similar sturdy material.

Your background should be a neutral gray or even black to accentuate your image definition. If, however, you wish to produce certain color effects, then Chapter 25 discusses the choice of varied color backgrounds. To conveniently change these colored backgrounds, purchase a number of large desk blotters which are available in many colors. These are flat and require little storage space.

Black-and-white film may be stock enlarged to jumbo size (approximately postcard size) while your transparency or Kodacolor negative may be enlarged or duplicated.

With dental photography, your problem is one of extreme close-up. The focal frame is needed for the very short distances.

Lighting for dental casts is very important. The problem of photographing white on white is a very delicate procedure. The author's method is to place the plaster of paris cast on a white surface. Then, use the bounce light method (Chapter 23) while all other room lights are turned off. While your exposures may be long, your lighting will be very even so that no part of the white cast will reduce a burnt-out highlight. The negative will print to a neutral gray tone and the gum line will be easily seen.

A great deal of routine may be eliminated by utilizing your X-ray marker for an information source of the subject. With your marker, you will have the subject's number, date, etc. When your picture is returned, file it together with your other records, but in its own separate envelope. The envelope should be seamless because many adhesives that are used for center sealing of the paper may eventually attack the emulsion.

Scientific photography in general may be practiced with your present camera equipment, some lights, and a few simple accessories. The results will be excellent if you follow the Safe-Set recommendations to simplify your clinical routine. If your medical photography is easy and produces good results, you will do more of it. The more you do, the greater the benefits that you will derive from it. But you must keep your methods simple in order to eliminate the possibility of error. This can be done with the Safe-Set Method.

Filter carrying kits

above: Focal frame for medical use
below: Focal frame for tilting

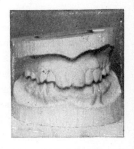

A dental cast.